Photo Credits

All photographs taken by Patrice Halley, with the following exceptions:

Pages 16 to 21: © Canadian Coast Guard Collection, all rights reserved

Page 99: © Maryse Leroux

Pages 242 - 243: © Solomon Krueger

Map design: © Philippe Brochard

Foreword introduction: Pascale Pontereau

Graphic designer: Ann-Sophie Caouette

Scanner operator: Mélanie Sabourin

Editor: My-Trang Nguyen

Canadian Cataloguing in Publication Data

Halley, Patrice

Sentinels of the St. Lawrence: along Quebec's lighthouse trail
Translation of: Les sentinelles du Saint-Laurent
1. Lighthouses - Saint Lawrence River. 2. Lighthouses - Quebec (Province).
3. Lighthouses - Saint Lawrence River - Pictorial works. 4. Lighthouses - Quebec
(Province) - Pictorial works. I. Title.

VK1027.S24H3413 2002   387.1'55'09714   C2002-940443-6

Government of Québec – Tax credit for book publishing – Administered by SODEC.

The publisher gratefully acknowledges the support of the Société de développement des entreprises culturelles du Québec for its publishing program.

We gratefully acknowledge the support of the Canada Council for the Arts for its publishing program.

We acknowledge the financial support of the Government of Canada through the Book Publishing Industry Development Program (BPIDP) for our publishing activities.

© 2002, Les Éditions de l'Homme,
a division of the Sogides Group

All rights reserved

Legal deposit : second quarter 2002
Bibliothèque nationale du Québec

ISBN 2-7619-1713-8

Exclusive distributors

- For Canada and the United States:

MESSAGERIES ADP*
955 Amherst St.
Montréal, Québec
H2L 3K4
Tel.: (514) 523-1182
Fax: (514) 939-0406
* A subsidiary of Sogides Ltée

- For France and other countries:

VIVENDI UNIVERSAL PUBLISHING SERVICES
Immeuble Paryseine, 3, Allée de la Seine
94854 Ivry Cedex
Tel.: 01 49 59 11 89/91
Fax: 01 49 59 11 96
Orders: Tel.: 02 38 32 71 00
Fax: 02 38 32 71 28

- For Switzerland:

VIVENDI UNIVERSAL PUBLISHING SERVICES SUISSE
P.O. Box 69 - 1701 Fribourg, Switzerland
Tel.: (41-26) 460-80-60
Fax: (41-26) 460-80-68
Internet: www.havas.ch
Email: office@havas.ch
DISTRIBUTION: OLF SA
ZI 3, Corminbœuf
P.O. Box 1061
CH-1701 FRIBOURG
Orders: Tel.: (41-26) 467-53-33
Fax: (41-26) 467-54-66

- For Belgium and Luxembourg:

VIVENDI UNIVERSAL PUBLISHING SERVICES BENELUX
Boulevard de l'Europe 117
B-1301 Wavre
Tel.: (010) 42-03-20
Fax: (010) 41-20-24
http://www.vups.be
Email: info@vups.be

For more information about our publications,
please visit our website: **www.edhomme.com**
Other sites of interest: www.edjour.com • www.edtypo.com
www.edvlb.com • www.edhexagone.com • www.edutilis.com

Sentinels
of the St. Lawrence

Patrice Halley

Sentinels of the St. Lawrence

Along Quebec's lighthouse trail

Translated from the French by
Michael Ballantyne and My-Trang Nguyen

For sailors lost at sea

For lighthouse keepers who have devoted
their lives to guiding the way

For Maryse, who one day led me to the banks of the St. Lawrence

Foreword

For 20 years "morningman" Joël Le Bigot unfailingly roused Montrealers from their slumbers. By turn, he amused them, indulged their imaginations, dressed up bad news in a comforting halo. With his warm-hearted chuckle and wrinkly, teasing eyes that smiled behind the microphone, the radio host brightened many a chilly morning. And then one fine day, out of the blue, he decided to follow his own dream. On board a friend's catamaran, he crossed the Atlantic, forsaking Quebec for his native France and the magnificent coast of Brittany. And so it was that the sea slowly and quietly entered his bloodstream, dulled as it was by years of city living. He had left it all behind for life on board a freighter bound for the world... Let's hear from the man himself.

Now that's a splendid idea, generous, long-anticipated. To pay homage to these great beacons of light and their keepers. In so doing, we also remind ourselves and our fellow countrymen – living too far away from our coasts and our islands – that the Mighty River is also, if not first and foremost, our "land," dating back to 1534. Because, sad to say, our eyes are more often turned southward and toward the interior rather than outward to the ocean. Even those who live in the little coastal villages, with a lighthouse in full view, albeit from the back, associate it with distant danger, farther out, on the horizon. Yet, they have often fallen asleep to the soft and melancholic sound of the foghorn.

All the same, who hasn't dreamed, while walking along the north and south shores, or vacationing in the Gaspé or Natashquan, about those curious souls who worked as lighthouse keepers. Who hasn't wondered where they hailed from, why and how they succeeded in cutting themselves off so completely from the outside world. And there they remained in the depth of winter, so high above the ground (but what a view!), those lonely lifeguards for seafaring folk.

It took self-sacrifice and great courage to place oneself at the service of others' lives. And so we owe it to them to make a concerted effort to preserve what remains of our heritage. They gazed on the sea in all its beauty, perhaps regretting that they had never set sail themselves. They saw the sea in turmoil, thanking heaven that they had never been at its mercy.

But no doubt one needs to have been out on the water and, in the evening, after a rough trip or a diffucult crossing, to have caught sight of that light that tells us, long before the scent of flowers and of the earth, that land is close — but not too close — to understand its value. Perhaps it was necessary to have experienced the reassurance that these tall protectors represent — heralding the heart-warming prospect of homecoming — to understand their charm and relevance, and to hope that they will continue to stand and be protected.

Do go to the riverside one evening, and study the light signals. You'll want to be a keeper yourself.

Certainly one can, as did the French poet Jacques Prévert, blame those lights for the deaths of many birds. But they are above all a lifeline for sailors. It's therefore up to us, now, to safeguard them.

It disturbs me to watch the fruit of 200 years of marine history simply disappear. It's easy to forget that Quebec has had a rich seafaring past, as the lighthouses bear witness. Hundreds of years of history, architecture, engineering, lanterns and mirrors, cannot be dismissed with a mere wave of the hand.

A hearty thank-you and bravo, then, to all those who invite us to pay more attention to their elegance, beauty and uniqueness. Let's seize the opportunity to affirm that we are a part of this history, that the river is also our "homeland."

JOËL LE BIGOT

A brief history of the lighthouse

Ever since our primitive ancestors learned to make fire, we have used artificial light to travel through the darkness in safety and confidence. In man's endless quest for new frontiers, the sea has always presented one of his greatest obstacles. In this contest with the elements, nothing captured the imagination of early mariners quite like the structure whose beacon helped guide them through the perils and deep loneliness of the open sea. And so the long history of marine navigation and the lighthouse are intimately linked.

Records show that the first lighthouse was built by the Egyptians in 300 B.C. on the island of Pharos, near Alexandria. Throughout antiquity, and until the dawn of the first millennium, lighthouse construction was scrupulously recorded in numerous documents dealing with marine navigation. From the Middle Ages to the Renaissance, and during the centuries that followed, European history was marked by warfare and trading activity that took place along coastlines and at sea. The power of nations rose and fell depending on the strength and reach of their fleets, as did the fortunes and reputations of those families whose names were linked to maritime commerce. No doubt Christopher Columbus, one of the world's most famous mariners, may have found inspiration for his historic voyages at the foot of a lighthouse. After all, his uncle, Antonio Colombo, had been the keeper of the Genoa light.

As a general rule, European lighthouses were erected by powerful trading rivals such as England and France to help their seamen gain safe entrance to their ports. Some were built in order to impress foreign navigators with the grandiose scale of their architecture: the Cordouan lighthouse in France, for example, erected by Louis de Foix in 1611, or England's Eddystone light, built in 1755 by John Smeaton.

In North America, the development of lighthouses and other navigation aids coincided with the birth of the colonies. The first light was erected in 1716 and helped guide merchant vessels into Boston harbor. The second light, built in 1733 by the French garrison at Louisbourg in Cape Breton, was destroyed by fire, then rebuilt before British guns demolished it in 1758. By 1800, there were 16 lighthouses in the fledgling United States, augmented annually by an average of 10 new ones.

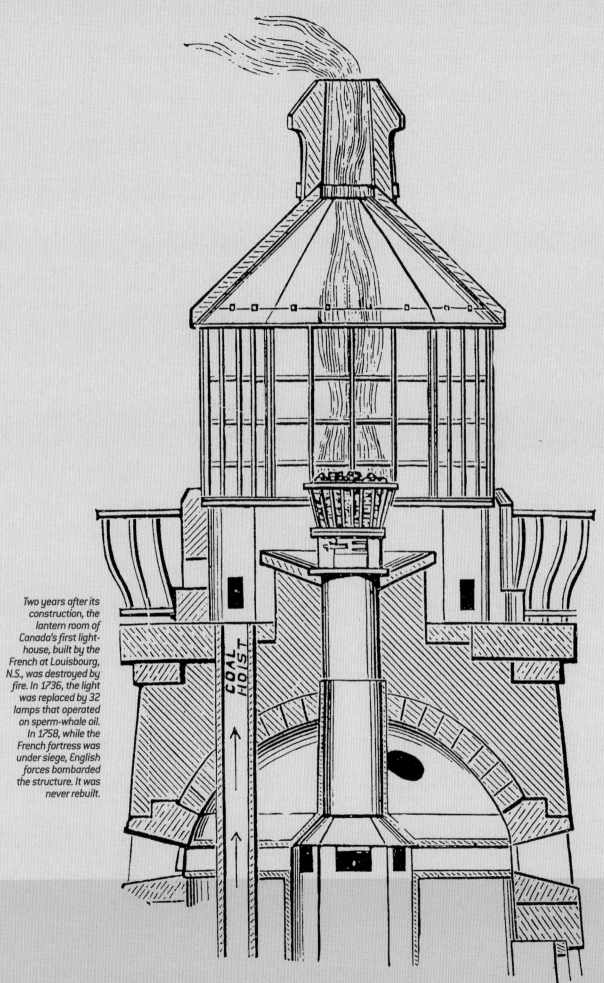

Two years after its construction, the lantern room of Canada's first lighthouse, built by the French at Louisbourg, N.S., was destroyed by fire. In 1736, the light was replaced by 32 lamps that operated on sperm-whale oil. In 1758, while the French fortress was under siege, English forces bombarded the structure. It was never rebuilt.

For more than a century, lightships were used as temporary measures at different locations on the river before they were replaced by permanent structures. Lightship Nº 3 was assigned to Île Rouge, while the famous Nº 7 (later called Nº 20) marked Haut-Fond Prince, at the entrance to the Saguenay River. The keepers on board those ships were professional sailors, accustomed to the pitching, rolling and fury of the sea.

In 1848, the lighthouse at Île Rouge replaced lightship Nº 3. Even though living conditions for the keepers, henceforth accompanied by their families, were easier on dry land, it remained a spartan existence and required great courage.

Meanwhile in Quebec, there was no comparable system for guiding mariners through the treacherous waters of the St. Lawrence, mainly because Lower Canada's colonial administration had no budget for developing navigation aids. Finally, in 1805, the government established an organization called Quebec Trinity House, modeled after Trinity House in London. The new entity was charged with organizing and establishing a network of lighthouses and other navigational assistance on the St. Lawrence. In 1807, the first lighthouse arose on Île Verte It was to be the only light to sweep the river until 1830, when Pointe-des-Monts on the Côte-Nord got its own station. The following year, a light was erected at Pointe Sud-Ouest, on the island of Anticosti, at the astronomical cost of $33,000. In 1835, it was the turn of Pointe Est (Pointe Heath), whose lighthouse cost $25,135. In 1843, a stone pillar was erected near Québec City, called Pilier Sud. In 1848, a second pillar was built on Île Rouge.

But it wasn't until 1857 that the colonial administration — under combined pressure from several maritime trading companies and the railway magnate Hugh Allan, head of the Montreal Ocean Steamship Company — agreed to endorse the construction of a more complete guidance system. As ever, the St. Lawrence posed enormous dangers for navigators. In 1857, four important lighthouses were built in Canada, among them the Pointe Ouest light on Anticosti, and the Cap-des-Rosiers light in the Gaspé. The latter was designed by John Page, chief engineer of Public Works, and built by François Baby.

Construction proved difficult and enormously expensive, but in 1858 both lights were illuminated for the first time. The Pointe Ouest light, which at a height of 34 meters rivaled its companion at Cap-des-Rosiers, cost $50,000. Cap-des-Rosiers was one of the most powerful lights in Canada at the time. Its optical equipment, manufactured in Paris by the renowned firm of Barbier, Bénard and Turenne, was installed by French technicians, replacing an antiquated seal-oil burner.

Although built on the coastline, as was often the case in Quebec, the lighthouse at Cap de la Tête au Chien was – and still is – one of the most remote and inaccessible sites along the St. Lawrence's north shore.

Quebec's first lighthouse, on Île Verte, housed lamps that still operated on seal oil, although by the mid 19th century it had become largely symbolic. It wasn't until the century's end that the province's electrical network was sufficiently developed to equip light stations with powerful filament lamps. The era of wavering light intensity was gone for good. With the advent of wireless transmission in 1904, mariners were finally assured of what had, up till then, been only a dream: a sense of safety.

After casting light over coastlines around the world, saving countless lives since time immemorial, lighthouses finally gave way to automation and the introduction of more effective navigation aids. Slowly they sank into obscurity. Yet, their symbolic value as guideposts and carriers of light is still firmly present in the popular imagination.

Lighthouses belong to our historical and cultural heritage and deserve to be celebrated. They are witnesses to the technological progress of the late 20th century and the long adventure of human achievement. At night, when villages sleep and sailors stand watch in the wheelhouse, the lighthouses still converse one to another in those bright flashes that gleam on the mirrored waters of the St. Lawrence. Does anyone still pay attention?

Neighboring the light at Cap de la Tête au Chien, the Cap au Saumon lighthouse sports a different architectural style. Unfortunately, the tower and the original wooden buildings have now gone, taking with them an important part of this romantic and special site.

Lighthouse keepers occasionally welcomed visitors, as here at Cap au Saumon. Yet, there were places where the loneliness of the keeper and his assistant proved too great an ordeal for most people to take on, with or without their families.

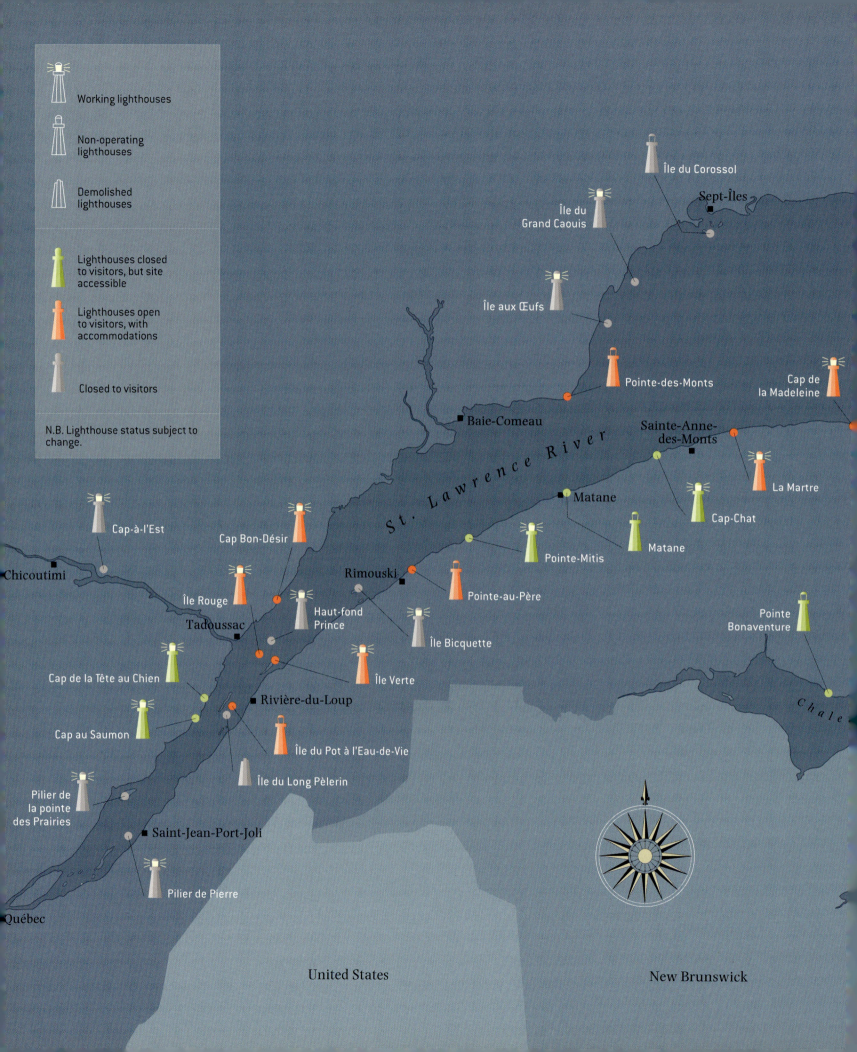

From Québec to Tadoussac

Every five seconds, the emerald-green light at Cap de la Tête au Chien flashes over the coastal mountains of Charlevoix. Then, with one generous burst, it sweeps over the mighty river.

Cap au Saumon

Located westward of Saint-Siméon, and even though it's a coastal lighthouse, Cap au Saumon is an isolated place. An almost hidden road brings adventurous hikers to the site. Standing on the grounds of the current lighthouse, which was built in 1955, you can watch the belugas that come to dally with the small pleasure boats.

Bathed in autumn's lively colors, the lighthouse now stands abandoned. Despite its special status, this heritage site risks being completely forgotten. It opened as a summer attraction for a number of seasons after having been renovated by the Corporation de Développement des phares du Saint-Laurent. However, the advent of the Manoir Richelieu's casino unexpectedly changed the "nature" of the region's tourist activities and so the lighthouse now faces tough, if not unbeatable, competition. In the foghorn building, a dusty mini-museum devoted to lighthouse history still awaits its first visitor. To attract people who are eager for a different kind of weekend escape, the corporation's former director, Robert Gilbert, tried to develop a first-class vacation center on the site. Plans included a spa, classical music concerts and candlelight dinners. But owing to lack of funds, the dream of the man who, for a short time, became the white knight of lighthouses has sadly petered out.

LATITUDE: 47° 46' 13" N ■ LONGITUDE: 69° 54' 21" W ■ MUNICIPALITY: SAINT-FIDÈLE DE MONT-MURRAY ■ HEIGHT: 14 METERS ■ HEIGHT ABOVE SEA LEVEL: 25 METERS ■ RANGE: 20 NAUTICAL MILES ■ FLASH: 15 SECONDS

Cap de la Tête au Chien

Driving along Highway 138, a sharp-eyed driver will notice a brief flash of light glinting from the peak of a distant knoll overlooking the coast at Saint-Siméon. It is the Cap Chien lighthouse, one of the most secluded on the entire north shore. At the foot of the granite cape, the river's current is compelled to bypass the cape and flows with unusual power. In the past, the keepers used a long crane to pick up or unload supplies. Nowadays, all you need to do is get up enough courage to jump straight from the boat onto the steep rock, a sometimes hazardous exercise. Next, the visitor has to climb 325 wooden steps leading to the lantern room where you can finally relish the 180-degree panorama over the river. André Lavoie and Pierre Lemay know a few things about this staircase — in the summer of 1999 they rebuilt the whole structure. Thousands of hammer blows to assemble before the steps were ready to lead one to heaven, or hell!

The sheer isolation of lighthouses can be disturbing, but when you find yourself in a place like Cap de la Tête au Chien, any sense of uneasiness is replaced by a feeling of fascination. Sitting on a rock, lost in contemplation of a river already salty but not yet broad enough to be called "the sea," the onlooker can follow the comings and goings of the belugas or the regular passage of ocean-going container ships. And then, in his

---

LATITUDE: 47° 54' 41" N ■ LONGITUDE: 69° 48' 23" W ■ MUNICIPALITY: SAINT-SIMÉON ■ HEIGHT: 11.6 METERS ■ HEIGHT ABOVE SEA LEVEL: 63.1 METERS ■ RANGE: 13 NAUTICAL MILES ■ FLASH: 5 SECONDS

You don't make a call at Cap Chien for the fun of it. As one can see, a human chain is needed simply to transport supplies to the summit.

solitary state, the watcher may be abruptly wakened from his reverie by the appearance of an enormous creature surging from the depths. Startled, he jumps to his feet, steps back from the edge, before realizing that he has had the rare privilege of seeing one of the river's unrivaled creatures — a fin whale, its mouth agape and dark eye gleaming, bursting to the surface in search of microscopic prey.

Thousands of hammer blows before the steps were ready to lead one to heaven, or hell!

Right: Located between the river and the mountains, the lighthouse at Cap de la Tête au Chien is sole monarch of the Charlevoix coast.

Haut-fond Prince

In 1860, the Prince of Wales' ship *Hero* was stranded on a reef east of the Batture aux Alouettes light buoy, at the confluence of the Saguenay and St. Lawrence rivers. To warn seamen of the dangerous reef, a lightship – christened *Prince Shoal* – was anchored near the spot the following year. As one lightship succeeded another, seamen were safely guided for more than a century. Not until 1961 did the Ministry of Transport decide to replace the *Prince Shoal* lightship with a lighthouse. Hydrographic studies were carried out over the next two years – made difficult by currents, winds and fog that prevented divers from expediting their work. The foundation was constructed in a dry dock and towed to the designated shoal, just off Tadoussac, where it was subsequently filled with 2400 tons of gravel and 24,000 bags of cement. In 1964, the huge and powerful xenon beacon lighted up for the first time, its 300,000-candlepower beam illuminating the river at the rate of four flashes every 10 seconds.

As a northeaster blew up the river, 10-meter-high tongues of water were often seen licking the lighthouse tower, affectionately called *toupie* [spinning top] by the locals. Before lighthouses were automated, keepers vividly recall the fear of being sequestered for days on end whenever Mother Nature misbehaved. Christmas Day 1966 was just such a time.

LATITUDE: 48° 06' 30" N ■ LONGITUDE: 69° 36' W ■ LONGITUDE: 69° 36' W ■ HEIGHT: 22.8 METERS ■ HEIGHT ABOVE SEA LEVEL: 25.3 METERS ■ RANGE: 20 NAUTICAL MILES ■ FLASH: 2.5 SECONDS

Muffled up in their survival suits, tourists on a whale-watching cruise discover a "spinning top" in their path.

For three days, waves as high as 15 meters pounded the pillar relentlessly. It had been built to withstand waves half as high, and by the third morning, the windows shattered and blew away. Water poured through, even penetrating the five-centimeter thick steel emergency door protecting the heating system. Paralyzed by cold and sheer terror, the keepers sent out their first distress call: "Please call Québec. The water's everywhere. It's like a river in here. The whole structure is shaking like mad. Our lives are in danger!" The message was picked up by the lighthouse keeper at Pointe Noire, who quickly relayed it to Québec. The storm forced the endangered keepers to wait another agonizing 24 hours before a coast-guard helicopter was able to land and evacuate them. It was a Christmas that Claude Fraser, Yvanhoé Gagnon and Roger Lagacé will never forget.

"Please call Québec. The water's everywhere. It's like a river in here. The whole structure is shaking like mad. Our lives are in danger!"

Automated in the 1970s, the Haut-fond Prince lighthouse is said to be haunted by a ghost who sometimes sets off the foghorn or switches on the lights at night. Now officially "retired," the last pillar lighthouse in the St. Lawrence still stands guard, lonely and abandoned, over the shoal. One day, perhaps, an enterprising businessman will convert it into a whale-watching station, and spare it from almost certain demolition. Located just off Cacouna, the pillar lighthouse at Île Blanche did not get a reprieve. It was dynamited in the early 1980s.

Right: One of the last remaining pillar lighthouses in Canada, Haut-fond Prince resists the ravages of nature as best it can.

Île Rouge

By Maryse Leroux

A few nautical miles off the river town of Tadoussac, far from tourist venues and the restless crowds on the quays, there is an island that few people know about. Its presence there is geological testimony to the immeasurable forces of the glaciers. The island appeared about 12,000 years ago after the glaciers had advanced and the Goldthwait Sea had dried up. It rests on a coastal shelf between the Appalachian and Laurentian mountain chains, facing the mouth of the Saguenay River, in a place where the Laurentian Channel makes an abrupt U-turn. There, the waters are swept by complex currents, brought about by a combination of powerful tides and the confluence of freshwater from the Saguenay and saltwater from the gulf. The Coriolis force can be felt up to that point and, for the sailor, the crests of the wild waves formed by the meeting of the waters in this spot are an unforgettable sight.

Samuel de Champlain is thought to have named the island Île Rouge because of the round, reddish pebbles that cover the rock. Oriented southwest and northeast, the island is not especially big, measuring about 600 by 250 meters. At low tide, a huge foreshore, 14 times longer than the island itself, comes to the surface at the northeast tip. Seals enjoy these rocky strands, but the banks are also a well-known navigation hazard, endangering mariners in good weather and bad. For more than 150 years,

LATITUDE: 48° 04' 09" N ■ LONGITUDE: 69° 33' 16" W ■ MUNICIPALITY: TADOUSSAC ■ HEIGHT: 17.8 METERS ■ HEIGHT ABOVE SEA LEVEL: 19.8 METERS ■ RANGE: 16 NAUTICAL MILES ■ FLASH: 10 SECONDS

After a final stroll along the shore, Robert Gilbert turns his back on an "old friend," the Île Rouge lighthouse. Now he must leave it to the mercy of wind and tide.

lighthouse keepers and their families lived here, cut off from the rest of the world. They helped to make things safer on the river and took care of many shipwreck victims. Living conditions were harsh in the extreme and each year the keepers sought permission from Quebec Trinity House to leave for the winter.

Just as every island has its private store of mysterious and foreboding tales, so too does Île Rouge. On November 8, 1860, for example, the diary of keeper W. Gilbert Lindsay, contains the following entry: "The headless body of the former keeper was found at 10 o'clock in the morning at the western head of Isle Rouge."

Living conditions were harsh in the extreme and each year the keepers sought permission from Quebec Trinity House to leave for the winter.

Since navigation aids were automated in 1988, the small, century-old lighthouse, built of brown stone imported from Scotland, has rapidly deteriorated. The keepers' houses have also fallen into disrepair. After a number of underwater diving expeditions in the area, Robert Gilbert, Jean-Marc Darveau and Patrice Deschênes — all keen marine anthropologists — took a personal interest in the island. In order to safeguard the site, they set up an association called the Centre d'interprétation et de mise en valeur de l'Île Rouge (CIMEVIR). After lengthy renovations,

Île Rouge offers the visitor comfort and solitude, with salt-tanged air and seabirds into the bargain.

the Hostellerie de l'Île Rouge welcomed its first guests in 1999. But for the men who had tried hard to give this special place a new lease on life, the reward was short-lived. At the end of the following summer, the complex logistics of running the inn had exhausted their operating budget. The "innkeeper-sailors" were obliged to hand over the oars to an entrepreneur with deeper pockets.

Today, life on the island is very different from that known by the keepers of old. Only the sound of waves breaking over the reefs and the cries of seabirds disturb the silence. From 1848 to 1960, the lighthouse only operated during the navigation period, from April 1 to December 15. The light itself, originally equipped with catoptric reflectors and 24 oil-burning lamps, had a range of 12 nautical miles. It was modified a number of times as technological advances dictated. The light continues to alert navigators to the presence of the sandbars, but its warning signal has been replaced by a bulb powered by solar energy. There are those who claim that lighthouses are no longer necessary, but for Robert Gilbert, the man who rescued the Île Rouge lighthouse from oblivion, letting go of the light and the island was as heartbreaking as saying goodbye to an old friend.

Above: Karina Laliberté's delicate violin spices up the already fiery words of Simon Gauthier, storyteller par excellence, before a spellbound audience.
Left: Martin Chouinard presents one of his culinary creations.

A stone lighthouse has stood on Île Rouge since 1848. For years, with the soles of their feet literally "half in the water," lighthouse keepers had only these few inhospitable acres on which to stretch their legs.

By Jean Cloutier

Profession:
St. Lawrence river pilot

Late on this particular afternoon, I happen to be strolling on the Plains of Abraham in Québec City. They were named in honor of Abraham Martin, who was born in France in 1589 and arrived in Canada at some point during the 1620s. He was pilot to Louis XIII and, as such, is considered to have been the first river pilot on the St. Lawrence. I'm a pilot myself and, within the hour, I'll be embarking on a ship coming from the port of Montréal. I'll be relieving the pilot who brought the ship down from Trois-Rivières, and I'll guide it as far as Les Escoumins. After I leave, the ship will continue on its way to Europe.

The transfer is made facing the city. The pilot boat bobs up gently to the ship's hull as it stays on course. An accommodation ladder is lowered from the guardrail, and I scramble up quickly. As soon as I reach the wheelhouse, the departing pilot gives me a short briefing before disembarking himself.

The ship is not a fast one, and as a result the rising tide slows us down significantly in the Île aux Coudres passage. All told, the trip will take us 10 to 12 hours. During the age of sail the same journey would have lasted several days. That's not surprising because of the frequent and sometimes lengthy stops along the way. Unfavorable winds, contrary tides, fog and the dark of night were added factors that obliged the pilot to drop

anchor and wait for conditions to improve. These days, however, with the help of on-board electronic positioning equipment, bad weather or other problems seldom force ships to stop. Constant vigilance is required, nonetheless, because instruments can break down or, worse still, transmit inaccurate information causing ships to run aground, helped, as it were, by their own technology. For this reason, I normally use visual means while I'm on duty. This gives me an opportunity to check the instruments for accuracy – and ascertain their margin of error in case they need to be used in fog, rain or snow.

I make some course changes in the waters off the depot at Pointe de Lauzon in order to head for Saint-Laurent-de-l'Île-d'Orléans. Passing abeam this little wharf, I file a radio report with the traffic dispatchers in Québec. They tell me that I'll encounter two ships between here and the next communication point, that there's a buoy out of position in the channel and that the lower leading light at Saint-Michel is out.

The next stretch of river between Saint-Laurent and Cap-Tourmente splits into two navigable channels. The north channel is 16 nautical miles long and, at 305 meters wide, is the narrowest part of our piloting sector. Here, the navigator has at his disposal a system of beacons and buoys in order to avoid shoals and other lurking obstacles.

In the days of the old French regime, this passage was booby-trapped with sandbanks. It was seldom, if ever, used because it was so tricky to navigate. However, one morning in 1759, the English fleet made it as far as Québec. Captain James Cook had taken surveys and drawn up charts which allowed the British ships to pass through a channel scorned by the French. The north channel soon became a new route and, year after year, it grew increasingly important, despite the fact that sailors preferred the south channel. Today, annual dredging operations maintain the north channel at a minimum depth of 12.5 meters. Now supertankers weighing more than 150,000 tons move through the same channel where, 250 years ago, pilots dared not venture aboard vessels weighing only a few tons.

At it exits this beaconed channel, the river broadens as far as Île aux Coudres. My job grows easier. I take advantage of this short respite to talk about winter. Hereabouts, even with a rising tide, the ice can be two miles wide, propelled by the current up to this funnel-shaped entrance that is half a mile wide. The ice then starts to pile up, blocking the entire navigable portion up to the foot of Petite-Rivière-Saint-François. It creates a spec-

For pilots like Yves Pelletier, who is busy guiding the Lovisa Gorthon — a Swedish container ship — life on the St. Lawrence is not always a long, calm journey.

tacular sight for skiers on the massif, giving them the impression that they can continue their downhill run right into the middle of the river. It's a very different sight for the pilot, who finds himself imprisoned aboard his ship, searching for cracks in the ice and places where the ice is thin enough to make progress despite the semi-solid state of the St. Lawrence.

We have now reached the pillar lighthouse at Île aux Coudres — the first of its kind on the voyage that is not a metal tower. Before this pillar was built on the sandbank, the Department of Marine and Fisheries placed a lightship in the area. They had to keep relocating the floating seamark for three long years before they found a secure construction site.

Here, the current created by the rising tide is very strong and slows the ship down considerably. I need to make a number of course changes in order to get round Île aux Coudres and point the ship toward Cap-aux-Oies. It wasn't so long ago, at a time when schooners monopolized the river, that they often stopped before reaching this point and started off again as the tide rose in order to benefit from its natural propulsion. Anyone who dared to tackle the tide head on simply stayed in the same place, since the speed of boat and current were virtually the same.

Changing course at Cap-aux-Oies, I've completed half the voyage — 60 nautical miles from Québec. Another 60 and we'll reach Les Escoumins. On the rocky point I can make out a metal tower capped with a rotating light. This modern structure replaced the original lighthouse that was built in 1876 by the same firm.

The 1960s were an unhappy decade for many of Quebec's lighthouses. Conventional political wisdom decreed that whenever it cost more than $130,000 to renovate a lighthouse, it had to be replaced by a new grid-type tower. As a result, several old lighthouses were pulled down. That was how we lost the lighthouse at Cap-aux-

Oies, and others at La Grande Île and Île du Long-Pèlerin. Fortunately, some were saved, the lighthouse on Île du Pot à l'Eau-de-Vie (Brandy Pot Island) among them.

From Cap-aux-Oies to the mouth of the Saguenay, the river widens a little. But this isn't the time to relax, because sailors can still fall afoul of the traps that the St. Lawrence conceals along its course. Keep in mind that there are more than 85 islands and islets between Québec and Pointe-des-Monts, not to mention shoals, submerged rocks, and narrower channels which in some places create currents as powerful as seven knots. Added to these natural obstacles are tidal movements that, four times a day, alter water levels all the way to Trois-Rivières, even though the city is 1500 kilometers from the Atlantic Ocean. In fact, from Sept-Îles, the tidal wave takes about an hour to reach the mouth of the Saguenay River and five hours to reach Québec. Afterward, it takes seven hours to reverse its flow, hourly affecting the direction and speed of the currents as changes in the tide dictate.

Passing between Pointe-au-Pic and Haut-fond Morin, one can't help asking whether the shoal, or any other rock in the river named after a real individual, owes its name to a sea captain or a pilot who got stranded there. That's the case with Haut-fond Prince, so named after a ship carrying the Prince of Wales ran aground on the shoal in 1860. As a matter of fact, maritime charts and pilot experience have probably improved after each disaster — a shoal, a sandbar or a sly counter-current was often discovered *after* navigators heard a *boom* beneath the hull. Such hard-earned knowledge has been passed down from generation to generation, all the while being augmented and brought up-to-date. So much so that in order to qualify as a pilot today, a candidate needs more than his master's papers and several years' experience — he must also serve an intensive two-year apprenticeship to learn all the tricks of this highly specialized trade.

Our progress continues. We're now off Cap au Saumon, which got its first lighthouse in 1894. The existing structure dates from 1954. It is almost identical to the famous lighthouse at Peggy's Cove in Nova Scotia. Cap au Saumon is not as accessible, however, and can't be photographed as easily as its companion light in the Maritimes. Later, we go by Cap de la Tête au Chien and its own lighthouse. This tiny tower was built on a rocky

Despite the new satellite positioning technology used in modern navigation, seamarks like the pillar at Pointe de la Prairie — indicating the approaches to the sandbank at Îles aux Coudres — still serve pilots as visual aids for lining up a ship's course.

escarpment, allowing it to beam its light 63 meters above sea level. Very often we can catch sight of its light while we're embarking at Les Escoumins, 30 nautical miles away.

We're approaching the entrance to the Saguenay; the passage will take us between the lighthouse at Haut-fond Prince and the one at Île Rouge. This has always been an awkward and dangerous section to navigate. The currents are powerful and their thrust carries you either toward Île Rouge, or Batture aux Alouettes.

So it's not surprising that the first lighthouse on the St. Lawrence was put up in this part of the river. The Île Verte lighthouse began its long and brilliant career in 1809. For 21 years it was the only light on the St. Lawrence. At that time, it wasn't hard for mariners to identify a light on a dark night and against a dark background as well. Today, I defy anyone to spot the Île Rouge lighthouse amid the myriad lights coming from the city of Rivière-du-Loup.

Passing by Haut-fond Prince, we have to make radio contact with the station at Les Escoumins. The spindle-shaped pillar that indicates the shoal allows it to act as an icebreaker. It was the last lighthouse built by the Canadian Coast Guard in the Laurentian region. Twenty-four years later, in 1988, it was the last lighthouse to lose its keeper. Since then all the lighthouses on the St. Lawrence have been automated and the profession of keeper is now extinct in Quebec.

The last leg of the voyage takes place in the kingdom of the great whales. Indeed, throughout the summer I've had the good luck to meet these formidable creatures on every trip. During the winter, on the other hand,

Headed for the Great Lakes, the Lovisa Gorthon *approaches the pillar light at Haut-fond Prince.*

The pilot boat from Les Escoumins comes alongside the Orsula, allowing the pilot to come aboard.

ice floes are a more common sight, despite the fact that very little ice forms between the Saguenay and Les Escoumins. This liquid expanse in the otherwise frozen river is easy to explain. Across from Les Escoumins the water depth varies from 200 to 300 meters and the river bottom rises steeply to 30 meters at Haut-fond Prince. The difference in depth and the changes in the tides create vertical currents that keep the water surface in constant motion, thus preventing the ice from forming or building up — a phenomenon known as polynya. Partly for that reason, in 1961 the embarkation station for pilots was moved from Pointe-au-Père on the south shore to Les Escoumins on the north shore, since it was necessary to find a place where the water was open in order to facilitate the transfer of pilots during the winter.

The Cap Bon-Désir lighthouse is the last to show off its winking lights, as I'm leaving the ship just three and a half nautical miles further on. I start to slow the ship down as the pilot boat approaches. I make some changes in the ship's course so as to give me shelter from the waves and the swell. My littler water-taxi snuggles up to the hull, I thank the captain as I give him information about the course he'll be taking and the traffic he'll encounter.

I step down, feeling a little tired after the long voyage but satisfied with the job that's been done. I've just piloted one of the 7000 ships that transit the St. Lawrence River each year.

From Tadoussac to Sept-Îles

The landscape around Pointe-des-Monts changes at the beckoning of the tides. At sundown, as the water rises, the St. Lawrence regains its command over the land and flaunts its majesty.

Cap Bon-Désir

One fine summer day, a group of children sit around on a bluff overlooking the St. Lawrence River, listening attentively to the words of a few Parks Canada naturalists. Stories of old king Neptune and his undersea realm hold the young audience in thrall. Suddenly there's an outcry: "There she blows! It's a fin whale!" In a flash, the children have taken off, scattering like sparrows over the pink rocks of Cap Bon-Désir.

A stone's throw from the lighthouse bearing its name, the cape itself is a vestige of the Pre-Cambrian shield. It has a platform overlooking the sea, where hundreds of visitors congregate every year, from mid-June to mid-October, to watch marine mammals swim in the underwater trenches near the shore. Compared with passengers on whale-watching boats, these land-based observers are a relaxed lot, free from seasickness and other worries. They bring their own picnics, and when a beluga or a porpoise surfaces, only "oohs" and "aahs" disturb the quiet atmosphere, a far cry from the frenzied picture-taking that inevitably occurs on a boat.

The cape attracted visitors long before ecotourism came to the area. As long as 8000 years ago, seal hunters frequented its weathered, well-polished rocks. Traces of their campsites, carved-quartz tools and seal bones have been found not far from the present-day lighthouse.

LATITUDE: 48° 16' 19" N ■ LONGITUDE: 69° 28' 07" W ■ MUNICIPALITY: BERGERONNES ■ HEIGHT: 10.67 METERS ■ HEIGHT ABOVE SEA LEVEL: 44.5 METERS ■ RANGE: 18 NAUTICAL MILES ■ FLASH: 5 SECONDS

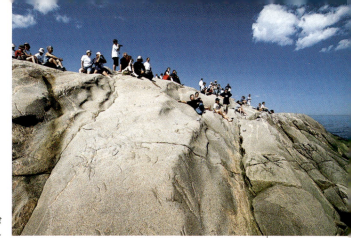

Cap Bon-Désir offers a magnificent platform for surveying the sea.

Emitting one last blow, the finback swims slowly away toward open water. Then, with a curve of its gigantic body — its ebony back glistening in the sunlight — the whale vanishes into the river depths. No longer distracted, the children come back and the naturalists finish their story without further interruption. A strong smell of iodine scents the air. People gather

As long as 8000 years ago, seal hunters frequented its weathered, well-polished rocks.

to talk, others drift away, some in the direction of the lighthouse — by way of a shady path snaking from the hilltop all the way to the sea — to visit the foghorn room. Soon a new group of visitors will arrive, picnic baskets and binoculars in hand. As with the previous group, they will scan the horizon for that telltale sign, that distant blow. And so life goes on at Cap Bon-Désir, on a Sunday afternoon.

Above: Between two whale spouts, children and their parents learn a little more about the ecology of the St. Lawrence. Left: Dressed in a fresh coat of paint, the lighthouse at Cap Bon-Désir overhangs the river under a cloudless sky.

Pointe-des-Monts

At Pointe-des-Monts, the north shore bends at an angle, allowing the St. Lawrence to relax a little before becoming part of the open sea. In 1826, 17 years after the construction of the Île Verte lighthouse, the eminently respectable Quebec Trinity House took the initiative to expand the network of navigation aids. Its governors dispatched John Lambly, who would later be appointed captain of the port of Québec, to choose a location for a new lighthouse. Pointe-des-Monts overlooked a treacherous part of the river, where a number of shipwrecks had already occurred. Lambly decided that it was an ideal spot to set up a light that would guide ships into the entrance of the estuary.

Work on the stone lighthouse began in July 1829. At first builders used local granite but, during the later stages of construction, blocks of limestone were transported by boat from Montréal because they were lighter to handle and easier to cut than the granite stones. While all this was proceeding, John Lambly was under threat from legal proceedings, notably by William Lampson, a merchant who owned trapping and exclusive trading rights with the native people over the entire north shore, and also by the cartographer, Henry Wolsey Bayfield, who declared that Lambly's site was not in fact the real Pointe-des-Monts. Construction work on the small island, located to the east of the actual Pointe-des-Monts, was by

LATITUDE: 49° 19' 37" N ■ LONGITUDE: 67° 22' 14" W ■ MUNICIPALITY: BAIE-TRINITÉ ■ HEIGHT: 30 METERS ■ HEIGHT ABOVE SEA LEVEL: 35 METERS ■ RANGE: NO LIGHT

then too well advanced to reconsider the venue. In 1830, an octagonal copper lantern was imported from England. It was installed at the top of the tower and, in September of the same year, Pointe-des-Monts officially became the second lighthouse on the St. Lawrence. Until 1960, the lighthouse was only accessible by sea. After 134 years of loyal and effective service, it was downgraded by the Ministry of Transport in December 1964.

For three generations, between 1872 and 1954, various members of the Fafard family succeeded one another as keepers of the light. But it was thanks to Jacques and Marie-Berthe Landry, the last keepers in a long line, that the lighthouse escaped demolition and was transformed instead into a museum dedicated to Quebec's maritime heritage.

Above: Between squalls, Jean-Louis Frenette and Eileen Yacyno, accompanied by Fred, their faithful golden retriever, enjoy a short cruise along the shore at Pointe-des-Monts. Right: You can read time's passing on the steps of the lighthouse at Pointe-des-Monts, engraved on the stone by the incessant comings and goings of the keepers.

From atop its seven stories, the oldest light on the north shore stands peacefully above the St. Lawrence. Two broad stripes of red break the flow of the white column that rises between the wild coastline and the open waters of the gulf. Worn down by the constant comings and goings of the keepers who maintained the lantern's 13 parabolic reflectors, the stone steps of the spiral staircase today convey the visitor on a journey back in time. Deep in the heart of the structure, sheltered by its two-meter-thick walls, the old registers and the keepers' personal effects quietly reveal, floor after floor, the evidence of an often difficult past. Every so often, a breath of air, bearing salt on its tongue, furtively touches the visitor. Somewhere a door bangs. One has the feeling that the shades of former keepers still inhabit this place and, aware of their importance for sea-faring folk, continue to watch over the lighthouse.

For his part, Jean-Louis Frenette, a geography professor and an enthusiastic "managing keeper" of the light, chugs calmly along the shoreline

Among the different pieces in its collection, the lighthouse-turned-museum at Pointe-des-Monts offers a journey through the life and times of its early keepers.

in his little outboard motorboat. Whenever he has a free moment, which is not often, he likes to take off with his companion, Eileen, and Fred, their golden retriever. Together they drift along, hugging the banks of the St. Lawrence, in search of what Jean-Louis calls "the emotional impact that you can find there, face to face with a timeless landscape." In fact, aside from the light station and a few houses, little has changed. This must have been the way Jacques Cartier first saw it — barely a soul in sight, covered in trees and peat bogs that, in mid-August, produce a bumper crop of juicy blueberries, making pickers and hungry black bears happy. One almost expects to encounter a tall ship proceeding upriver, sails proudly unfurled, or perhaps a sea serpent that, as legend has it, lurks in the waters off the point.

Pointe-des-Monts overlooked a treacherous part of the river, where a number of shipwrecks had already occurred.

Frenette guides the boat as his mood takes him. Surprised by a shower, as calm as a Breton sailor, he takes refuge in a small cove. His life seems to revolve around the lighthouse. From June to September, in a house adjacent to the old tower, he welcomes tourists. On the ground floor, a restaurant offers excellent meals, while on the floor above the old keepers' rooms provide travelers with a good night's sleep and a view of the sea. In the distance, a storm rolls over the horizon and beneath an inky blue sky, the river, to the delight of children who stroll along the ancient granite shore, sweeps the air with veils of foam that rise in vain toward the clouds.

Right: The oldest lighthouse on the Côte-Nord contemplates its aged reflection in a tidal pool. Following pages: After an ebb tide, the land is reclaimed from the river, much to the delight of ramblers.

Île aux Œufs

On their way to attack Québec in August 1711, some ships of the 88-strong fleet under the command of Admiral Sir Hovenden Walker were overtaken by fog and broke up on the reefs at Île aux Œufs. The story is that Admiral Walker had forced a French-Canadian — the renegade captain, Jean Paradis — to pilot his squadron. The discontented Paradis deliberately led the ships to ruin on the reefs. That day, the admiral lost not only the greater number of his men, but also his fiancée and his honor. As a consequence, Québec was spared. A result clearly due to the intervention of the Blessed Virgin, say the more pious; a simple case of accident, others argue. But, if Captain Paradis was himself the responsible party, then why invoke the name of the Virgin or blame it on accident? Is the story itself just a legend? Whatever the case may be, since that time, on certain evenings in the month of August, an English frigate can be seen, moored far out to sea. Local folk will tell you that it's Admiral Walker, coming to visit his fiancée who perished on that long ago night. Folklore is alive and well on the Côte-Nord. In 1871, an 11-meter-high octagonal wooden lighthouse was built by the Department of Marine and Fisheries, an official body that replaced Québec's Trinity House. The keeper's quarters were attached to the structure. After several renovations, the lighthouse was finally replaced in 1950 by a concrete tower similar to the original but located at a slightly lower level.

LATITUDE: 49° 37' 19" N ■ LONGITUDE: 67° 10' 31" W ■ MUNICIPALITY: RIVIÈRE-PENTECÔTE ■ HEIGHT: 10.7 METERS ■ HEIGHT ABOVE SEA LEVEL: 19.5 METERS ■ RANGE: 7 NAUTICAL MILES ■ FLASH: 6 SECONDS

Whatever the weather holds in store, the springtime kayakers will rendezvous on Victoria Day weekend.

A multitude of seabirds nest on the nearly two-kilometer-long reef, hence the island's name. But on this Friday in May, on the eve of Queen Victoria's birthday, only the faint sound of sand rolling under the ceaseless motion of the waves disturbs the still countryside. The river is slack. Every year a small group of friends from the Côte-Nord region get together here for a weekend of camping as well as a sea-kayaking excursion to the lighthouse. Marc and his family are the first to arrive, then Christian and Robert with Jessica, followed by Simon, Amélie, Marie-André, Mathilde, Bélinda. Soon more than 20 souls are busy pitching their tents while the children run along the beach. The ritual is well organized. While some campers sort the provisions or gather wood for the evening's bonfire, others grab their rods and go fishing. Like docile mounts, the kayaks are slid from car roofs

Like docile mounts, the kayaks are slid from car roofs toward the beach and the group soon embarks on the crossing.

Posing for a group photo. The springtime kayakers take advantage of the holiday weekend to hold a family get-together on Île aux Œufs.

toward the beach and the group soon embarks on the crossing. Because they are more experienced, Christian and Marc stay at the rear in case one of the small craft drifts toward open water. The river current is powerful hereabouts, and will quickly carry you far from the southern head of the island. Today, the gray skies don't lift and the picnic will be a chilly one. But more importantly, these friends are together once more before the start of the long summer season. They'll meet again when the capelin are running. Along the Côte-Nord, traditions are long-lasting.

Île du Grand Caouis

There is a light swell running on the river, as is usually the case, its grayish tones reflecting the color of the sky in the monochrome landscape. On this May morning, spring still seems a long way off on the Côte-Nord. The air is cold, but the blue whale doesn't seem particularly concerned, living as she does far below in the ocean's basement, surfacing only occasionally in order to breathe. They say she's blue, and yet not even the keenest observers can honestly say what her real color is. She was spotted entering the gulf in good company six days ago, and through that labyrinth of currents, has navigated toward what humans call the River. Oh, she certainly knows this body of water — that it flows in both directions and alters its flow every six hours. After all, hasn't she spent many seasons here, at first clinging to her mother's side for rich milk, then alone in search of adventure? She did stay away for a couple of seasons, but always comes back. This is where she, in turn, provided her own brood with milk and taught them to avoid the dangers lurking on the surface; where she guided other members of her species through the deeps known for their abundance of food. Today, however, the mammal seems old and careless, as though she were letting herself go. *Time to come up for air*.

LATITUDE: 49° 49' 35" N ▪ LONGITUDE: 67° 00' 21" W ▪ MUNICIPALITY: RIVIÈRE-PENTECÔTE ▪ HEIGHT: 10.7 METERS ▪ HEIGHT ABOVE SEA LEVEL: 45.1 METERS ▪ RANGE: 8 NAUTICAL MILES ▪ FLASH: 6 SECONDS

Looking mighty pleased with his prize, Elliot holds up two herring gull eggs.

"A blue whale!" a little boy called Elliot exclaims. "A big one!" Carefully, Robert Gilbert alters the course of his zodiac. *No point in rushing*, the old sea dog thinks, maintaining the helm at 235. His crooked tuque, two-day old stubble and red-veined eyes betray the rum-soaked party of the night before. For her part, the old whale seems impervious to the engine's noise. Have the years deadened her hearing? But the boy's cry animates her. Whales no doubt can differentiate the sounds made by humans, their erstwhile killers. In the old days, a joyful cry could mean only one thing: that whale blood was flowing nearby. But that's no longer the case. On this morning, the animal appears to enjoy listening to Elliot, because she lingers a little longer on the surface. "It's spouting, it's spouting," Elliot calls out. "There's a whale, there's a whale!"

Oh, she certainly knows this body of water – that it flows in both directions and alters its flow every six hours.

Without a keeper today, the Île du Grand Caouis lighthouse looks utterly desolate. Built in 1927, the classic octagonal tower in painted concrete is abandoned. But you can picnic high up on the helicopter pad, all the while watching humpbacks and minkes pirouette far below, where the river merges with the gulf.

Right: The rock at Grand Caouis is a splendid promontory. Elliot and his mother, Sophie, watch a minke whale at play.

From Sept-Îles to Blanc-Sablon

The ornithologist on Île aux Perroquets has finished his day's work. His lantern's ghostly beam undulates through the Mingan darkness.

Île du Corossol

Jean-Baptiste-Louis Franquelin, the royal hydrographer, was sent to New France to map the colonies. It was Franquelin himself who drew up one of the earliest maps of the Côte-Nord.

Recalled to Paris in 1692, he left behind his wife, Elisabeth Auber-Franquelin, and eight of their 13 children. In 1693, after months of petitioning, Franquelin finally received the monarch's permission to repatriate his family aboard the *Corossol*, one of the vessels belonging to the royal fleet. That summer, the ship ran into a violent storm just off Sept-Îles, and sank. Except for the ship's pilot, the first mate, and a handful of sailors, there were no survivors. The *Corossol* vanished, like so many others before it, in the dark, cold waters of the St. Lawrence. It wasn't until 1694 that its sinking was confirmed. A recovery mission, organized by the Comte de Frontenac, governor of New France, and led by marine lieutenant Levasseur, yielded 12 cannon and four anchors – all retrieved from the river.

Marcel Galienne stepped cautiously along the path that led to the Île du Corossol lighthouse. As he proceeded, he disturbed a few seagulls that flew off, squealing at the intruder. Galienne worked as a lightkeeper at Corossol for 32 years. Although he kept a cottage on the island, tucked away in a sheltered cove, he hadn't returned to visit the lighthouse since leaving in 1988. Standing on top of the rock at the lighthouse base, he

LATITUDE: 50° 05' 20" N ■ LONGITUDE: 66° 22' 45" W ■ MUNICIPALITY: SEPT-ÎLES ■ HEIGHT: 12.8 METERS ■ HEIGHT ABOVE SEA LEVEL: 57.9 METERS ■ RANGE: NO LIGHT

inspected his old haunt. Overgrown by waist-high grass, the footpaths he alone had known so well no longer existed. With difficulty, he trudged on until he reached the lighthouse door. Glass from splintered windows cracked

Standing on top of the rock at the lighthouse base, he inspected his old haunt.

under his feet. He stretched out his hand toward the concrete structure, covered with chipped paint. He hesitated, then at the last moment, clenched his fist and pulled back his hand. Overcome by emotion, he looked up to the top of the empty tower. There was no light to be seen. Discouraged, he looked around at the sad state of the abandoned building. He had raised his family here, worked hard to look after everything and followed the strict

Marcel Galienne, former lightkeeper on Île du Corossol, traces a path through the tall wild grasses that today cover the abandoned island. In the Galienne family, the job of keeper was handed down from father to son, a tradition that came to an end in 1988, following the automation of lighthouses.

rules laid down by his old employer. It was a beautiful July day. Still, the waves were six meters high and the ride back on the zodiac was bumpy. Marcel Galienne hasn't been back to the lighthouse since.

The *Corossol* vanished, like so many others before it, in the dark, cold waters of the St. Lawrence.

Completely abandoned, Corossol is now home to an impressive colony of migratory birds which invade the island's 57 hectares every year. As many as 12,000 petrels, common eiders, guillemots and black-legged kittiwakes have the place to themselves, amid a cacophony of bird calls, languages as strident as they are incomprehensible. The lighthouse has been transformed into a tower of Babel.

The lighthouse on Île du Corossol stands bleakly atop its cliff, with neither light nor keeper.

Île aux Perroquets

In a letter written in 1633, Samuel de Champlain mentioned the existence of a fragment of rock 360 meters long, 2.6 nautical miles off a sandy coast.

Long before the village of Longue-Pointe ever existed, Île aux Perroquets was anchored in the Jacques-Cartier Strait, along with other fragments of ancient rock that formed the Mingan Archipelago. Spreading over 2.7 hectares, the island owes its name to a colony of Atlantic puffins dubbed *perroquets de mer* [sea parrots] by the early European seafarers.

In 1872, Henri de Puyjalon, the 32-year-old son of a French marquis, emigrated to Canada. A cultivated gentleman, with a penchant for books about natural history, as well as an intrepid hunter and indefatigable hiker, de Puyjalon set out to thoroughly explore the Côte-Nord, writing accounts of the region's flora and fauna. He was fascinated by the Mingan Archipelago, and in 1888 became the first lighthouse keeper at Île aux Perroquets. De Puyjalon devoted the rest of his life to the study and protection of nature. Together with his wife, Angélina Ouimet, he traveled tirelessly over the entire region. After he died in 1905, he was buried according to his last wishes — at a spot overlooking the sea on Île à la Chasse, with the ghostly monoliths of Mingan watching over his resting place.

LATITUDE: 50° 13' 04" N ■ LONGITUDE: 64° 12' 24" W ■ MUNICIPALITY: LONGUE-POINTE ■ HEIGHT: 12.3 METERS ■ HEIGHT ABOVE SEA LEVEL: 24 METERS ■ RANGE: 12 NAUTICAL MILES ■ FLASH: 5 SECONDS

Today, Jojo is the only flesh-and-blood gannet on Île aux Perroquets. No matter how hard the bird flaps its wings as it tries to respond to the strident calls of its fellow gannets, they pay him little heed. These gannets are clearly a conservative bunch, preferring to settle down on the same patch of barren rock every year. The other seabirds on the island — Atlantic puffins, black-legged kittiwakes and Arctic terns — are more accommodating, and yet, the little colony that used to nest on Île aux Perroquets has now left the cliffside. In the past few years, the Quebec-Labrador Foundation, the Audubon Society and the Mingan Island Cetacean Study have organized a program to reintroduce gannets to the island.

During the summer, ornithologists use the Île aux Perroquets lighthouse as an outpost from which to monitor the island's bird population. They've converted the ground floor into a kitchen, the first floor into an office and the outside parapet has become an observatory. Each morning, as the first rays pierce the windows of the little cabin that serves as their private quarters, Christophe Buildin and Laura Del Giudice set off on their daily routine. As they cross the small island on their way to the lighthouse, its paint chipping and flaking, the cold dampness rising from the river penetrates their warm turtleneck sweaters. After a frugal breakfast, Christophe climbs to the top of the tower, binoculars and guidebook in hand, while Laura sets up her 50 hand-painted decoys on a cliffside,

Every morning Laura Del Giudice sets up "her" gannets. Right: Unlike the gannets, the pretty puffins rarely make noisy neighbors.

With a field guide in hand and binoculars at the ready, ornithologist Laura Del Giudice surveys the occasional "feathered visitors" on Île aux Perroquets.

in the hope of luring gannets back to the site. She then turns on a recording of gannet calls. Until dusk falls, Laura and Christophe scrupulously check the presence of different birds, stopping only to answer questions posed by the occasional visitors.

Convinced that gannets have only limited intelligence, the scientists believe their strategy will be sufficient to attract the birds. So far, however, only Jojo has taken the bait. It has decided to settle down on the island, no doubt because its plastic neighbors have given him no problems.

The Côte-Nord is born of fire – the granite rim of the North American continent – while the Mingan Archipelago is born of water; its islands are the fragments, the shards of an ancient land that slowly settled at the bottom of the Silurian seas.

FRÈRE MARIE-VICTORIN, *Flore de l'Anticosti-Minganie*

On this day, Île aux Perroquets is cloaked in a snaking fog that undulates capriciously with the morning breeze. Riding the small white motorboat that takes her there, Marie Collin-Kavanagh stares at the lighthouse. It seems to play hide-and-seek, now exposed by the sun, now wrapped in a scarf of white cloud. It's been 12 years since Marie last set foot on the island. Her husband was once the chief lightkeeper and that was where she raised three children. Today, she's visiting her old home – the stone embankment, the field of wildflowers and the pebble beach that were

In memory of her deceased husband, lighthouse keeper Robert Kavanagh, Marie Collin-Kavanagh poses with their wedding picture.

once part of her daily landscape. As the boat moors alongside the algae-coated pier, Marie exclaims happily: "This is God's wharf!" Her eyes fill with emotion because this is a homecoming of sorts. The lighthouse has been completely automated since 1981. In her diary, Marie once wrote: "What small creatures we all are in the face of such an immense ocean, and on this tiny gem of an island in the gulf that God gave us." Walking along the familiar path across the island, she remembers: "One summer, we spent eight consecutive days in a closed, opaque world. That was the longest time that we ever went without seeing the sun." She stops mid-way, then turns off toward a promontory where a small white statue of the Virgin Mary stands. She places her hand on the pedestal, closes her eyes and lets her thoughts drift back in time.

Each winter, navigation stopped toward the end of December or the beginning of January, at which time Robert Kavanagh and his assistant customarily shut down the lighthouse, and took the dangerous crossing

to Longue-Pointe. On January 9, 1954, after the order arrived to close the lighthouse, the keeper and his assistant hastily complied, then launched their boat before the waters iced over. The temperature was particularly cold that winter and the island was caught in a frozen stranglehold. On the way, the motor stalled and the men were forced to row back to the island. But they didn't make it all the way and the little boat was quickly trapped by the ice. In the hours that followed, the two men, now prisoners of the river, the ice and the cold, feared for their lives. It was at that point than Robert began to pray to the Virgin, begging her to lead them safely to shore. In return, he promised to erect a statue on the island-cape to protect all navigators. Finally, a channel opened up before them. "We couldn't see the island or dry land, and we couldn't continue because of the ice," Robert reported in a radio message once he was back on the island. The two keepers had to wait until January 25 before two hardy souls from Longue-Pointe, Gérald Collin and André Dérosby, were able to rescue them.

From sunrise to sunset, Christophe Buidin makes careful notes of his ornithological observations.

The tide rises surreptitiously. As we get ready to leave, a zodiac slowly pulls up at the dock to pick up the Mingan Island Cetacean Study research team. They have to return to the mainland to fix a mechanical problem.

"We couldn't see the island or dry land, and we couldn't continue because of the ice."

Richard Sears, a whale specialist and biologist and the team's director, has decided to stay behind. Ever on the lookout for whale spouts, he rushes up the tower to survey the gulf with his binoculars. Her eyes still misty with memories, Marie Kavanagh takes her place on the boat as her son-in-law, Marius, steers it toward the far shore. As she drifts away from "her island," Arctic terns, like a troupe of tiny ballerinas, come squealing to salute her, before flying off into the infinite azure sky.

In earlier times, all the keepers had at their disposal to reach the island was a small motorboat. Today, inhabitants of Longue-Pointe-de-Mingan take the shuttle used by enthusiastic tourists, who turn up to watch the Atlantic puffins.

Petite Île au Marteau

A couple of nautical miles off Havre-Saint-Pierre, at the heart of an oddly shaped string of islands bearing picturesque names, stands a little lighthouse that could easily pass unnoticed.

Here, at low tide, the east wind can be treacherous. As powerful tidal currents push the swells toward the shore, the breakers are known to have caused inattentive or inexperienced sailors to veer off course, heading instead for one of the many reefs dotting the cold, dark waters. On October 15, 1867, in the course of a single night, five schooners were stranded on the Mingan Archipelago.

Eventually, a lighthouse was at built on Petite Île au Marteau. It made its début on a clear August evening in 1915. Late in the day though it certainly was, it nevertheless helped avert more shipwrecks. In return for a meager salary of 200 dollars, the keeper made sure the seal-oil lantern was well maintained and promptly lit each night. No longer in service, the white tower still carries signs — for the benefit of fishermen and yachtsmen — indicating the entrance to the channel where river traffic is particularly busy. It is a place where cargo ships and kayakers cross paths, not to mention the occasional ocean liner. At night, it is a metallic tower, willowy and soulless, that now marks the archipelago for passing vessels.

LATITUDE: 50° 12' 04" N ■ LONGITUDE: 63° 33' 31" W ■ MUNICIPALITY: HAVRE-SAINT-PIERRE ■ HEIGHT: 11.6 METERS ■ HEIGHT ABOVE SEA LEVEL: 13.7 METERS ■ RANGE: NO LIGHT

In front of the old lightkeeper's house, the capaillou-bearing "pilgrims" listen intently as actors recount the history of the island and its light.

Starting July 1, the *Perroquet de Mer* leaves Havre-Saint-Pierre every Sunday at dusk on a mystery tour. It is probably the only boat in the archipelago sailing back into the past. As a veil of mist descends, blurring the pale contours of the coasts, the captain steers the craft past Île du Havre, and heads for Petite Île au Marteau. Bundled in warm blankets at the bow, the children look forward happily to whatever surprises the special outing will bring, while their parents chat quietly in the stern.

In the flickering light of the lanterns, the procession winds along a narrow path and takes on a phantasmagorical mood.

In the old days, the inhabitants of Havre-Saint-Pierre used to adorn processions and children's sleighs with homemade lanterns called *capailloux*. They were simple contraptions — you took a discarded tin, punched a few holes in the sides and inserted a candle. The origin of the name is uncertain. Some people believe that the French naturalist Henri de Puyjalon imported the expression from France in the 19th century, others consider it an Acadian invention. Since the word is heard only in Havre-Saint-Pierre, linguists wisely label it a local usage.

Arriving at its final destination — Petite Île au Marteau as it existed "in 1937" — the *Perroquet de Mer* docks and the passengers disembark. The guides hand each one a *capaillou* and the nocturnal pilgrimage into the past begins. In the flickering light of the lanterns, the procession winds

At a bend in the path on Petite Île au Marteau, "pilgrims" discover that the life of an old-time lighthouse keeper, punctuated by wood gathering, the drying of codfish and maintaining the lantern, was far from a restful existence.

along a narrow path and takes on a phantasmagorical mood — moving shadows on the bushes, whispered sounds, nervous laughter. At a bend in the path, someone suddenly leaps out of the darkness. Startled, the nervous procession undulates like an immense caterpillar. But it's only a "bootlegger" on his furtive rounds. During the pilgrimage, the explorers get to meet Madame Simone, the local schoolteacher, Mr. Léger Cyr, the lighthouse keeper, his assistant, Grégoire, and his two daughters, Cécile and Anita. They tell the visitors about the island and what their daily lives are like.

For a few hours each year, hundreds of people revisit the past in this way. The return to the present day takes place around midnight, as the *Perroquet de Mer* heads back for the lights of Havre-Saint-Pierre, which glitter on the horizon. Filled with memories of another era, the explorers let themselves be rocked by the tidal currents as a meteor shower streaks across the sky.

By Marie-Claude Ouellet

The St. Lawrence – a river rich in resources

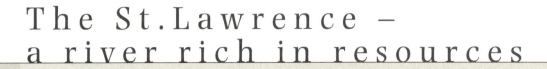

As a natural habitat, the St. Lawrence region is exceptional, home to thousands of plants and hundreds of animal species. As conditions along the shoreline change, so too does the vegetation. Where the level of water salinity reaches 1%, for example, sea grass will appear, and while certain species such as alternate-flowered spartina and glasswort thrive in salt marshes, others like American beach grass and beach pea favor sand dunes. Our forebears learned how to benefit from plants such as seaweed, sea-rocket and sea-plantain leaves, mountain cranberries and black crowberries. Silverweed, creeping savin and kelp were used to make medicines, and eel grass, once dried, helped insulate houses and iceboxes, wrap fragile objects, or pad horse collars, car seats and mattresses.

The St. Lawrence River is an abundant source of food and prime habitat for its animal population. The region's fauna is mainly found on and around isolated islands and lonely capes; in other words, those hidden places far from farmland and urban development. Interestingly, areas where the old lighthouses were built, such as Pointe-des-Monts, Île Verte, Anticosti and Île aux Perroquets, are excellent vantage points for birdwatching or for observing seals and whales. But the best location of all is underwater, where you can swim alongside creatures such as sponges, jellyfish, snailfish, sea urchins and many other species – less familiar perhaps, but no less fascinating. The key to the St. Lawrence River's abundance is largely to be found in its underwater topography and currents. Since the riverbed consists of abrupt peaks and valleys, the currents cause the ice-cold water at the bottom to rise in tandem with the riverbed, bringing with it large quantities of nutrients

Purple sandpipers make a gregarious stopover on Petite Île au Marteau before continuing their long journey south.

which, under the effect of sunlight, act as fertilizers, stimulating the growth of microscopic algae called phytoplankton. These plants, in turn, feed a host of small crustaceans that attract seals, seabirds, and whales – with tourists bringing up the rear. Areas where icy water rises include the stretch between Tadoussac and Grandes-Bergeronnes, the Mingan Archipelago and Pointe-des-Monts.

As a scuba-diving location, the South Seas have nothing on the gulf, alive as it is with equally attractive organisms, not to mention 300 species of crustaceans, 140 species of mollusk and 10 species of starfish. There are also 185 fish species – 87 of which are freshwater denizens, 80 saltwater and 18 diadromous; that is, fish that regularly migrate between fresh- and saltwater. Some 15 of these species, including the lake sturgeon, American eel and Atlantic cod, are endangered today as a consequence of overfishing. Fishing is a major economic activity in the estuary and Gulf of St. Lawrence, notably the Gaspé, Îles de la Madeleine and Côte-Nord. In fact, cod fishing had become so aggressive that it was suspended in 1993. Birds, too, thrive in the region, where as many as 115 species find refuge and plentiful food. During migratory periods, in the autumn and spring, almost a million snow geese congregate on the river's shores, not to mention the great blue heron, which has as many as 30 colonies scattered here and there. Incidentally, the Grande Île colony in Lac Saint-Pierre – home to more than a thousand nesting pairs – is the largest great blue heron colony in the world. Unlike the snow goose and the great blue, other shorebird species – including the bald eagle, Caspian tern and piping plover – are threatened by extinction, due to overzealous hunting, destruction of wetlands, egg harvesting and pollution. Steps have now been taken to safeguard these birds. On the Îles de la Madeleine, for example, fluorescent ribbons are tied around piping-plover nests to make sure that the eggs and baby birds are not crushed by hikers and all-terrain vehicles. To protect eider ducks in Basse-Côte-Nord, both spring hunting and egg harvesting have been drastically curtailed. The St. Lawrence constitutes a choice habitat for mammals, both semi-aquatic – like mink, otter, beaver and muskrat – and marine, like whales, seals, and dolphins. Of all the marine mammals that frequent the river, cetaceans are by far the most popular, as witnessed by the proliferation of whale-watching tours in recent years. The first excursion on the St. Lawrence was organized in 1971. Until then, the presence of whales in the area – considered to be one of the best observation sites in the world – was a well-kept secret. Tour operators quickly caught on, however, and today more than 50 boats offer trips to the St. Lawrence estuary, catering to some 300,000 tourists annually. The industry generates more than $40 million annually in the Tadoussac region alone.

Whale watching has become so popular that many people now fear the activity may disturb these peaceful creatures. An ecotour operator must first make sure that excursion boats respect the well-being of the whales. Unfortunately, this is not always the case. Seals are much less popular, although their pups attract several hundred ecotourists a year, flocking to the ice pack on the Îles de la Madeleine to see them at close range. The islands are the best spot in the world to approach the so-called whitecoats — baby harp seals less than 12 days old. Apart from the beluga, no one really knows just how many individuals of each whale species exist in the St. Lawrence. According to the most recent census, between 1000 and 1400 belugas currently inhabit the river, as opposed to between 5000 and 10,000 at the end of the 19th century. The dramatic decline is attributed to commercial hunting (finally banned in 1979) and chemical pollution. Necropsies have revealed that St. Lawrence River belugas suffered from an abnormally high incidence of lesions and tumors (often cancerous), in all likelihood a result of pollutants. Endangered today, the beluga has become a symbol of wildlife conservation.

Endangered ecosystem ▪ Four hundred years ago, Basque and Breton fishermen harvested cod and whales in the St. Lawrence. Later, it was the turn of European settlers to exploit the river's riches — fish, shorebirds, walruses, whales and seals. As long as it was practiced on a small scale, this kind of exploitation could proceed for a long time without damaging effect. The introduction of modern hunting and fishing techniques, however, dealt the resources a near fatal blow, and they quickly dried up. Unfortunately, it took a long time before anyone realized that the river's reserves should be exploited with greater restraint lest we harm the entire ecosystem. By then, another serious error had been made. Mistakenly believing that the river could

With their gaudily colored beaks, eyes underlined with a touch of "mascara," and plumage worthy of evening attire, Atlantic puffins justify their "sea parrot" nickname. In fact, they belong to the same alcidae family as the penguin.

automatically and indefinitely replenish itself, tons of pollutants – industrial, agricultural and municipal – were dumped into the river on a regular basis. Of all polluting agents, toxic substances such as mercury, lead, PAH[1] and PCB[2] have the most insidious, long-term effects. In fact, both PAH and PCB are known carcinogens. Certain pollutants turn up in the tissues of living organisms, while others accumulate in the sediments on the river bottom. If the sediments are disturbed – during dredging operations, for example – the pollutants rise with them, potentially harming fish and even human health as they permeate the food chain.

Pollution jeopardizes a host of activities, from recreational swimming to the harvesting of mollusks, considered unfit for consumption once they have absorbed and stored micro-organisms within their shells. And there's the fact that more than half the population of Quebec – about 3 million people – depend on the St. Lawrence for their drinking water. Maritime traffic poses another threat. A heavily traveled route to the Great Lakes – the agricultural and industrial heartland of North America – the St. Lawrence contends with heavy maritime traffic. Each year, thousands of container ships enter its waters – many loaded with oil or other potentially harmful products – increasing the odds of an accidental spill. Fortunately, the number of maritime accidents on the St. Lawrence has fallen by half in the last decade, thanks to the increasing use of GPS systems.

It's summer at Forillon National Park, and the whales come out to play. A finback swims alongside the shore at Cap Gaspé. In the distance, the lighthouse can be seen at the end of the cape.

1 PAH (Polycyclic Aromatic Hydrocarbon): toxic substances resulting from fuel combustion, waste incineration and the smelting of steel and aluminum.
2 PCB (Polychlorinated Biphenyls): mixtures of synthetic organic chemicals that were used in electrical, heat-transfer and hydraulic equipment, lubricants, pigments, dyes, carbonless paper, etc. Production was banned in Canada in 1980.

A harbor seal takes a sunbath beside the St. Lawrence.

On the other hand, the St. Lawrence's falling water levels may complicate the situation. In the past five years, rising temperatures and low precipitation have caused significant evaporation in the Great Lakes, reducing their outflow to the St. Lawrence. In 1998 and 1999, the water fell to its lowest level in 20 years, and the discharge rate fell from 30 to 40% below average. The situation has forced commercial vessels to offload some of their cargo before reaching the port of Montréal, with serious economic consequences. If global warming continues as expected, the average rate of discharge in the Montréal area may fall by half. This situation will have a disastrous impact on aquatic fauna, as well as on fishing, navigation and the quality of drinking water. It is a problem that greatly preoccupies environmentalists.

Among cetaceans frequenting the St. Lawrence, the humpback is the most exuberant showoff.

Having carelessly exploited the resources of the St. Lawrence and befouled its waters, we have finally realized what a fragile ecosystem it is. For 20 years, the government of Quebec has made great strides in water treatment. In 1980, for instance, 300 municipalities dumped raw sewage into the St. Lawrence. Since then, most have acquired water-treatment plants to filter the waste before it enters the river. Furthermore, toxicity levels of industrial wastes have greatly diminished. Still, much work remains to be done, especially with regard to agricultural pollution and snow disposal. Fortunately, more and more concerned citizens have joined to fight to save the majestic St. Lawrence.

From Québec to Sainte-Anne-des-Monts

The patriarch of Quebec's lighthouses has illuminated the St. Lawrence since 1809.

Île du Pot à l'Eau-de-Vie

In 1534, the European Renaissance was in full flower. Then, more than ever, England and France competed in their quest for a gateway to the Indies. While the English explored the Northwest Passage, the French king, François the First, entrusted a Breton pilot with a mission of discovery. With a single vessel and a crew of 61 men, Jacques Cartier sailed from Saint-Malo in search of a passage to India. He entered the Gulf of St. Lawrence, explored Newfoundland and the Îles de la Madeleine. But running out of time, he was forced to end his voyage near Anticosti and returned to France. A year later, again under royal charter, Cartier set sail once more. He left Saint-Malo on October 30, this time with three ships. He discovered the entrance to the St. Lawrence River and sailed all the way to Hochelaga, today the city of Montréal. There, he spent the winter with his men – all gravely ill with scurvy – and in 1536, they headed back to the mother country. During this return journey, it was probable that Cartier stopped at a small island to replenish water supplies. Today, the island is known by a delightful name: Île du Pot à l'Eau-de-Vie, dubbed Brandy Pot Island in English.

Jean Bédard leans over a bird's nest. Six fragile eggs, pretty in olive green, are resting in a warm bed of down and dry leaves. Delicately, he separates the eggs one by one and removes a handful of down from the nest. He nimbly picks out the few sprigs and wisps of straw that are caught in the feathers, then stuffs the down in his canvas pouch. That done,

LATITUDE: 47° 52' 15" N ■ LONGITUDE: 69° 40' 50" W ■ MUNICIPALITY: SAINT-ANDRÉ ■ HEIGHT: 11.9 METERS ■ HEIGHT ABOVE SEA LEVEL: 21.6 METERS ■ RANGE: NO LIGHT

With gentle hands, a down gatherer collects nature's offering. The harvest's ultimate objective is to protect the island and its eider ducks.

he carefully replaces the eggs, covering them with down and dry grass to conceal them from potential predators. Any minute now, the female eider will be back to tidy up her nest.

From May to July, close to 30,000 eiders migrate up the eastern seaboard to the many islands scattered in the St. Lawrence. In the lower part of the river, a flock of ducks have made themselves at home on Île du Pot à l'Eau-de-Vie and other nearby islands. With the help of private donations, Jean Bédard, a nature lover and biologist by training, acquired these ancient fragments of rock and turned them into a bird sanctuary. Today, Bédard reigns supreme over Île du Pot à l'Eau-de-Vie. To ensure peace and quiet for his protégés and to finance his environmental activities, he markets the down feathers harvested from his boarders.

Still the work is not quite finished, because more often than not, the feathers they have gathered are full of lice.

Jean Bédard is a hands-on manager, while an assistant keeps meticulous records of the state of the nests. As the harvesters go about their work, their comments can be heard in the wind: "Hatching in process." "No down in this nest." "Eggs hatching." Eagle-eyed, they have an uncanny ability to spot female birds as they take flight, thus indicating the presence of hidden nests. Harvesting feathers is hard on the body. When you're not bending over hundreds of times every hour, you have to slide under trees so as not to step on nests, or climb the rocks, and wade

After a long day's toil, Jean Bédard and his fellow down gatherers strike a pose in front of the little lighthouse on Île du Pot à l'Eau-de-Vie (Brandy Pot Island).

through swamps. Nest after nest, bush after bush, the harvesters continue their strange, monotonous litany: "Two hatchings, one incubation," "One hatching, one harvest," and so on. By the end of the day — which sometimes stretches late into the night — they're exhausted. Still the work is not quite finished, because more often than not, the feathers they have gathered are full of lice.

Clouds soon appear on the horizon and a north wind kicks up. By the look of it, a storm is imminent and Jean Bédard is worried, continually scanning the sky. The pace quickens. Everyone tenses up. The harvesters' backs bend lower and lower under the weight of their heavy bags. Then the sky darkens and the storm is unleashed. It's time for the harvesters to leave the island. Plunging through the waves, they squint through the spray looking for the light from Île du Pot à l'Eau-de-Vie that will guide them safely into port at Rivière-du-Loup.

Proud of its plumage, a male eider duck takes a siesta on the shore.

Gilles Rioux does some major housekeeping for his guests. In fact, the lighthouse tower makes an ideal eyrie from which to observe the island's birdlife.

The "Brandy Pot" lighthouse with its 10-meter high cylindrical tower is a unique feature on the St. Lawrence. Built in 1851, at a time when maritime accidents were frequent because sailors used wind power alone to propel their vessels against the tides, the lighthouse guided many a schooner going upriver, laden with wheat, millet or seal oil. Abandoned in 1964, the lighthouse became a target for looters and vandals. In 1985, both the island and the lighthouse were "rescued" by the Société Duvetnor Ltée, a non-profit organization founded by Jean Bédard and his friends, based in Rivière-du-Loup. In 1999, the Pot à l'Eau-de-Vie lighthouse was designated a "classified federal heritage building, in view of its exceptional surroundings, special architectural quality and historic value."

During this return journey, it was probable that Cartier stopped at a small island to replenish water supplies. Today, the island is known by a delightful name: Île du Pot à l'Eau-de-Vie, dubbed Brandy Pot Island in English.

One thing is certain. Thanks to Jean Bédard, the little lighthouse and the island, visible on the earliest maritime maps, will now carry on the history and tradition of welcoming seamen. Soon, 500 years will have passed since the first visitors stopped at Île du Pot à l'Eau-de-Vie to quench their thirst. To the great delight of yachtsmen and bird lovers – with whom Jean Bédard enjoys sharing the island's natural resources – the lighthouse has been converted into a cosy seaside inn.

From the top of the lighthouse tower, you can look out over the river at slack tide and see the nearby islands. Paul-Louis Martin points out to Marie de Blois the flash from the light at Cap de la Tête au Chien, gleaming in the distance.

Île Verte

Ever since its discovery, the St. Lawrence has been regarded as one of the most perilous waterways in the world. Daytime navigation proceeded visually, aided by river pilots, but at night, the river was plunged in darkness. In 1806, soon after Quebec Trinity House was given the task of establishing a network of navigation aids, the Lower Canada Parliament approved a light station project on Île Verte, at the junction of the Saguenay and St. Lawrence rivers.

Two London manufacturers — George Robinson and Brickwood & Daniels — were awarded contracts, the first to make the 12-sided copper lantern, the second to furnish the lighting apparatus, designed to operate either on seal or whale oil. On September 21, 1809, the *Gazette de Québec* published the following report: "As of today, the light on Île Verte will shine every night, from dusk to dawn, until December 15 inclusively." And so Quebec's first lighthouse was born. For 18 years, Charles Hambelton — the first keeper — meticulously tended the light, guiding ships safely away from dangerous reefs as well as the treacherous currents spawned by the Saguenay. When Hambelton died in 1827, the Île Verte light was still the only beacon to sweep the waters of the St. Lawrence.

In 1856, the station was augmented by two cannon that acted as fog signals. They boomed every 30 minutes whenever visibility on the river was reduced. In foggy weather, life on the island was hardly relaxing.

LATITUDE: 48° 03' 03" N ■ LONGITUDE: 69° 25' 27" W ■ MUNICIPALITY: NOTRE-DAME-DES-SEPT-DOULEURS ■ HEIGHT: 16.8 METERS ■ HEIGHT ABOVE SEA LEVEL: 16.5 METERS ■ RANGE: 19 NAUTICAL MILES ■ FLASH: 5 SECONDS

Like a theater curtain, the window of the little museum on Île Verte opens to reveal the oldest lighthouse on the St. Lawrence.

Hambelton was succeeded by Robert-Noël Lindsay, who in turn was replaced by his son, Guilbert, in 1867. Sadly, Guilbert's sons Guillaume and Thomas, aged 10 and 16 respectively, drowned after their small boat

They boomed every 30 minutes whenever visibility on the river was reduced. In foggy weather, life on the island was hardly relaxing.

capsized near the lighthouse. In 1888, Guilbert himself suffered a bad fall as he was repainting the lantern. Despite these misfortunes, the Lindsay family were to be linked with the Île Verte lighthouse for 137 years.

The lighthouse underwent many changes during its lifetime, notably in terms of automation in 1969.

The lighthouse underwent many changes during its lifetime, notably in terms of automation in 1969. As a result, its last keeper, Armand Lafrance, retired in 1972. Finally, in 1976, the light was classified as an historical monument and the municipality of Notre-Dame-des-Sept-Douleurs took

Above: Set up between land, sea and sky, the lighthouse on Île Verte has given comfort to sailors since 1809. Left: Today Gérald Dionne watches over the grand old ancestor of the river's lighthouses.

over responsibility as the owner. Today, tourists and local residents in search of a little peace and quiet can enjoy the island's bucolic landscape, hiking or biking amid fields of wildflowers. Islander Gérald Dionne is a self-appointed keeper today, welcoming his "one-night assistants" to the station's various buildings. A few local historians and lovers of the old tower have installed a modest museum in the ancient foghorn room, reminding visitors that the light station saved countless souls from shipwreck.

Gérald Dionne explains the working of the automated light to his visitors. Before the advent of electricity, oil, kerosene, and finally incandescent lamps were used.

Almost 200 years old, the Île Verte lighthouse still casts its brilliant beam into the night.

Île Bicquette

The fox trots up to the edge of the woods and halts for a moment, methodically sniffing the air. The scent of iodine emanating from the seaweed-covered shoreline tickles its nostrils, prompting it to search – vainly – for potential prey. Soon, the animal disappears empty-handed into the cover of the trees. Carried by the wind, the distant sound of a boat engine can be heard, disturbing the island's peace. A small aluminum boat glides swiftly into the dark waters of the Baie du Bic. As Marc Lapointe slips past Cap Enragé, a west wind begins to whip up the waves. Soaked by spindrift, he hunches up his shoulders, his hands numbed by the chill October squall. Marc instinctively knows the way between the barely submerged rocks along the Baie du Bic and the nearby islands. Once past "the Twins," he reckons, Île Bicquette can't be very far away. Today, he is going to shut down the island for the winter. Each year almost 15,000 common eiders arrive to nest on the island. After the incubation period, in May or June, Marc and his father-in-law, Patrice Thibault, move to Île Bicquette with their families, sharing a square kilometer of green space and stunted forest with birds and rabbits. Nature provides enough work for the two men. But the down-feather harvest is now over, and the ducks have left for warmer climes until next season.

Essentially composed of material the geologists call schist, Île Bicquette is part of the Appalachian range. Under the old French regime, the port of

LATITUDE: 48° 24' 55" N ▪ LONGITUDE: 68° 53' 34" W ▪ MUNICIPALITY: LE BIC ▪ HEIGHT: 20.1 METERS ▪ HEIGHT ABOVE SEA LEVEL: 34.1 METERS ▪ RANGE (WHITE LIGHT): 12 NAUTICAL MILES ▪ FLASH: 2 SECONDS ▪ RANGE (RED LIGHT): 5 NAUTICAL MILES ▪ FLASH: 6 SECONDS

Bic was used as a marine supply depot, where pilots changed ships and missionaries relaxed between their evangelizing efforts. With busy maritime traffic and no warning systems, many ships were lost in storms or came to grief on the reefs.

Like its companions at Île Verte, Pilier de Pierre and Île Rouge, the Île Bicquette light, erected in 1843, is part of the original network of lighthouses that commanded the St. Lawrence. The thick-walled, 22.3-meter-high circular tower was built with wood and stone. Inside the curved glass and copper sheathing of the dome stands a lantern manufactured by the renowned French firm of Barbier, Bénard and Turenne. At the foot of the lighthouse are two cannon, silent now after years of wear and tear. They are witnesses to a not-too-distant past, when their explosive chant led mariners safely through the fog.

They share a square kilometer of green space and stunted forest with birds and rabbits.

From 1927 to 1962, Ernest Thibault was the island's caretaker, followed by his son, Maurice. It was Maurice who closed the island in 1988 after the light was automated. In former days, Bicquette was inhabited from April 1 to January 15, when keepers returned to the mainland just before the river froze. Legend has it that in 1859, the boat carrying the first two keepers broke apart on the ice and the men drowned. The new keeper, a man called Fortier, was forced to winter over on the island. During his long, solitary confinement, he began to hear the rattle of chains and moaning sounds issuing from the tower. Terrified, Fortier rushed headlong from the island. He knew the crossing would be perilous, but sheer terror overcame the danger presented by the ice. Fortier was eventually found, paralyzed by terror and fatigue. He vowed never to return. Ever since, keepers no longer winter on Île Bicquette. As soon as he lands, Marc Lapointe takes off at a run to start work. Deliberately and matter-of-factly, he makes the rounds of the buildings, checking doors and windows. His inspection complete,

Just like its illustrious neighbor on Île Verte, the Bicquette lighthouse was built with wood and stone.

Like a safe, a steel door protects the valuable optical apparatus manufactured in France by the firm of Barbier, Bénard and Turenne.

Marc jumps back into his boat. Instinctively, he looks up at the old light. The weathervane has changed direction. The sky signals a storm, and so rain will be his companion on the return voyage. No sooner has the boat moved away from the shore than the fox reappears from behind a screen of dwarf balsams. Relieved by the man's departure, the animal resumes its quest – a prisoner on Bicquette until the first ice starts to form.

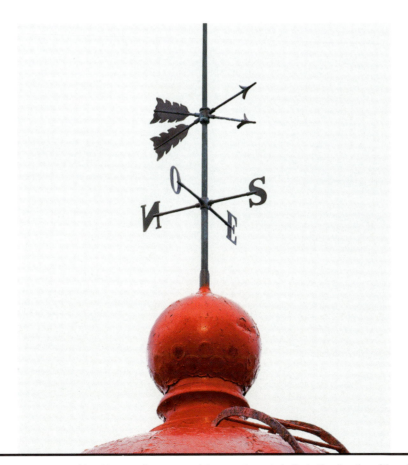

Bicquette's weathervane, unconcerned by old age or the ravages of time, continues to indicate the direction of the wind.

Pointe-au-Père

Today the young students at École du Bon Pasteur in Matane are going on an outing. Scarcely out of breath after climbing the 128-step spiral staircase to the top of the Pointe-au-Père lighthouse, Louis, Étienne, Fanny and Jean-Philippe rush into the lantern room. They press their noses against the Fresnel lens, caressing the sections of glass as though they were made of crystal. As the children look around the room, their guide relates the story of the lighthouse.

It began simply enough in 1800, with a fixed lantern installed on the roof of a house at Pointe-au-Père — considered an ideal spot for observing ships — by the Montreal Steamship Company. It wasn't until 1859 that a timbered lighthouse was built by the government of Canada. Eight years later, the structure was destroyed by fire and replaced by a wooden twin tower. Despite its 15-nautical-mile range, the new tower was soon considered obsolete in view of the ever increasing traffic on the St. Lawrence. Still, with river pilots preferring this lighthouse to the official station at Le Bic, Parliament finally passed a law, in 1905, designating Pointe-au-Père as the area's official pilot station. The decision took effect a year later, following the construction of a deep-water dock. In 1909, a 29.5-meter high concrete octagonal cylinder was built. Reinforced by eight buttresses, it could support an even more powerful light — a third-order Fresnel dioptric lens 5.2 meters high, with a range of 15 nautical

LATITUDE: 48° 31' 04" N ■ LONGITUDE: 68° 28' 06" W ■ MUNICIPALITY: POINTE-AU-PÈRE ■ HEIGHT: 27 METERS ■ HEIGHT ABOVE SEA LEVEL: 27 METERS ■ RANGE: 15 NAUTICAL MILES ■ FLASH: FIXED LIGHT

miles. The only drawback was that the mechanism had to be rewound every six hours. The lighthouse was finally automated in 1975.

On the night of May 29, 1914, at 1:20 a.m., the 14,000-ton transatlantic liner, *Empress of Ireland*, carrying 1477 passengers and crew, stopped at Pointe-au-Père to drop its pilot. The ship steamed on toward Liverpool when a thick fog bank enveloped the river. Forty-five minutes later, after reaching the shipping lane, the *Empress* altered course, heading toward the gulf. Moments later, it was struck by the *Storstad*, a Norwegian freighter. The 152-meter-long liner went down in barely 14 minutes, taking with it more than 1000 victims into the dark waters. Captain Henry Kendall remained on the bridge as his ship sank, but he survived. Today, the *Empress of Ireland* lies in 44 meters of frigid, treacherous water, a gravesite that only expert divers dare visit.

Today, the *Empress of Ireland* lies in 44 meters of frigid, treacherous water, a gravesite that only expert divers dare visit.

In 1974, the Point-au-Père lighthouse became a National Historic Site, no longer used as an operating light. As the 1980s dawned, its light was extinguished. The lens was then draped with a cloth cover until such time as the Musée de la Mer decided to restore the crumbling tower to its former glory.

Right: Through the lenses of the Pointe-au-Père light, one can't help making faces, technology notwithstanding.

After their visit, the schoolchildren make their way toward the spiral staircase, leaving a couple of youngsters in the back who seem to be in no hurry to leave. Pretending that the lighthouse is an interstellar spaceship, they are about to launch it toward a distant planet in search of more

In 1974, the Pointe-au-Père lighthouse became a National Historic Site, no longer used as an operating light.

adventure. Can anyone blame them? Certainly not the old lighthouse, almost a century old now, whose staircase vibrates every day under the feet of hundreds of enchanted children. But the voice of the schoolteacher is soon echoing through the cavernous concrete structure. Time for the children to come back to earth.

Pointe-Mitis

At the end of Lighthouse Road in Métis-sur-Mer, a line of rocks stretches into the sea. As upright and straight as a pillar, a lighthouse clad in white concrete and topped by a red cap, shines in the darkness. It's Pointe-Mitis. The 17-meter-high lighthouse tower warns sailors against hidden reefs, sharpened to a knife-point by the timeless movement of ancient ice sheets and the constant motion of the tides.

Built in 1874, on a piece of land belonging to John MacNider, the original light was replaced by the existing tower in 1909. The new lighthouse was part of a scheme by the government of the new dominion to make improvements in the network of maritime navigation aids, supplanting the old wooden lighthouses with concrete-built replacements. The Métis-sur-Mer light was one of the first reinforced concrete lighthouses in Canada. The property of the Canadian Coast Guard, the lighthouse is fully automated. The old lightkeeper's house and outlying buildings now belong to the local center for forestry research.

LATITUDE: 48° 40' 49" N ■ LONGITUDE: 68° 02' 02" W ■ MUNICIPALITY: MÉTIS-SUR-MER ■ HEIGHT: 17 METERS ■ HEIGHT ABOVE SEA LEVEL: 24.1 METERS ■ RANGE: UNKNOWN ■ FLASH: 7.5 SECONDS

Cap-Chat

Inside the small lighthouse perched more than 40 meters above the water, Sylvie Vallée installs a cannon on the upper deck of the 17th-century galleon, *Soleil Royal*. The model-maker's eye seems enormous as she peers through the magnifying glass. She picks up some wire with a pair of tweezers and, hand held steady, twists a rope that she then coils and places beside the cannon. Sylvie Vallée has already built a dozen models for the Musée du Fleuve: sailing ships such as *La Couronne* and the *Sovereign of the Seas*, but also early 19th-century cargo vessels like the *Harvey*. The construction of miniature ships and boats inside bottles was a popular hobby of the old lighthouse keepers, but at the Cap-Chat station, first built in 1871, there hasn't been a keeper for a very long time.

The current tower itself, a mere 10 meters high and today closed to the public, was built in 1909. The light is still working. Like many others, it was manufactured in Paris by the firm of Barbier, Bénard and Turenne. The keeper's house is now a museum and tearoom. The museum was the inspiration of Joseph Augustin Saint-Laurent, a man who loved everything to do with the sea. Its walls are decorated with seascapes painted by Lucie Gagnon. The lighthouse itself is set in the Jardin des Brumes [Garden of Mists], comprising nearly two kilometers of lovingly maintained paths and flowerbeds, all open to the public. The inhabitants of

LATITUDE: 49° 05' 20" N ■ LONGITUDE: 66° 44' 27" W ■ MUNICIPALITY: CAP CHAT ■ HEIGHT: 13.5 METERS ■ HEIGHT ABOVE SEA LEVEL: 41.4 METERS ■ RANGE: 15 NAUTICAL MILES ■ FLASH: 6 SECONDS

Cap-Chat have at last found a new use for their lighthouse. Popular belief has it that the name of this community and its cape comes from the shape of a large rock – resembling a seated cat – which the lighthouse overlooks. But toponymy and history suggest rather that the name was taken from one of Samuel de Champlain's lieutenants, a certain Chaste, who visited the site in 1691.

The construction of miniature ships and boats inside bottles was a popular hobby of the old lighthouse keepers, but at the Cap-Chat station, first built in 1871, there hasn't been a keeper for a very long time.

Right: The original optical system at Cap-Chat still revolves in a mercury bath but, as in many other lighthouses, the ageing system has begun to show signs of wear and tear. While it awaits renovation, the tower is closed to the public.

Shipwrecks and tragedies

Such is the beauty of the St. Lawrence River that it is easy to forget its crucial role in our nation's history. This majestic body of water quickly impresses visitors to its shores with breathtaking landscapes and remarkable flora and fauna; but few among us appreciate how dramatically it has shaped our past history or how deeply it has marked our sense of culture. Be that as it may, when you see those immense cargo ships ply its waters, propelled by gigantic screws, the importance of the St. Lawrence as a means of transporting goods deep into the interior becomes clear. But it is more than just a waterway, albeit one of the very few that — for a long time — permitted relatively quick access to the heart of Canada. For centuries now, our relationship with the river has changed considerably, shaped by discoveries, economic conditions, technological changes, wars, tragedies. Some of these changes may be difficult to discern today, though the countless shipwrecks found in the river itself are part of the evidence — vestiges of ships that once plied its waters, and in so doing were intimately linked to the lighthouses ranged along the shoreline.

For the Europeans, the St. Lawrence was pre-eminently an immense storehouse of riches to be exploited for their own benefit and development. Amerindians were already using the river to hunt seals, as archeological discoveries at the foot of the Cap Bon-Désir lighthouse have demonstrated. Even before Jacques Cartier arrived in 1534, Basque and French fishermen had discovered that the entrance to the Gulf of St. Lawrence, and the river itself, teemed with cod and whales. The Red Bay shipwrecks, found at the northern entrance to the Gulf, are witnesses to the 16th-century economic boom, when hundreds of ships braved the Atlantic crossing, hoping for a bountiful harvest of cod and whale oil. One of three known Basque galleons now rests near Saddle Island, where a lighthouse bearing the same name was later erected. The wreck was carefully excavated; the fact that many barrels still lay atop the oak timbers indicate that the oil-laden whaler sank during a sudden and violent autumn storm as it prepared to head home. Nearby, the wooden skeleton of the *Bernier* emerges from the icy waters, a stark reminder of the sudden violence of which these seemingly placid waters are capable. In the 1560s, it suffered the same fate as the Basque galleon.

The exploitation of the St. Lawrence continued unabated during the early 17th century, drawing cod fishermen and whale hunters up river. In the minds of the French explorers in particular, the river represented a gateway to an unknown land — the Indies, perhaps — filled with yet more wonders and riches. And so the adventurers set out enthusiastically, hoping to probe those mysteries, to cast their eyes on exotic places and creatures as yet unknown to European civilization. As time passed, this impetus took on a fresh meaning, attracting settlers

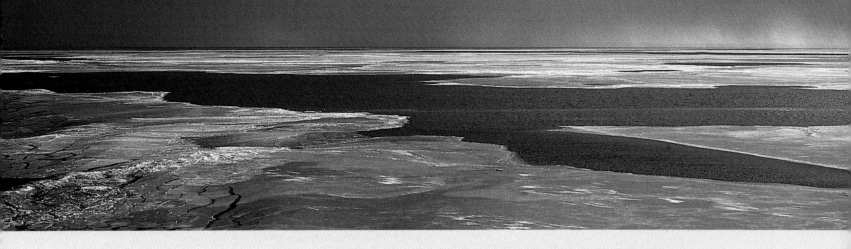

from France, eager to establish themselves in a new country where the prospects were unlimited and full of promise. The waters of the St. Lawrence were reached only at the end of an endless, often nightmarish passage. Once there, settlers found that their new homes clung to the edge of a vast, unknown continent beyond the river. Yet they understood that the waterway was in fact a vital artery in the geography of their new country, dictating the way land would be distributed and acting as a hub connecting the settlements. It also functioned as a kind of long-distance umbilical cord, linking the settlers to the mother country. It was on the St. Lawrence alone that the goods essential to the survival of the colony arrived, or failed to do so.

The presence of a rival colony quite literally next door, whose appetite for the same rich resources — Canada's fish-rich waters in particular — was becoming ever more evident, meant that hostilities were inevitable. The St. Lawrence became a war zone, a vast chessboard on which maneuvers and confrontations occurred for almost a century. A wreck discovered near Pointe-des-Monts — the site, incidentally, of one of the most charming lighthouses on the St. Lawrence — bears witness to the first of those confrontations. The ship was the *Elizabeth & Mary*, a small merchantman that set sail from Boston in 1690, part of a 32-ship expedition intent on capturing Québec City. Led by Sir William Phips, the men struggled upriver, eventually reaching Québec after much hardship and delay. Their ignorance of the implacable St. Lawrence proved costly. The water froze before they could seize the city, trapping them and sinking four of the ships. Personal belongings found at the wreck — leather boots, pipes gnawed up to the bowl, improvised lamps and various family mementoes — help to tell the story of men held prisoner by the river for almost three months. But the St. Lawrence was just as hard on its own people. Three years after the debacle of the Massachusetts expedition, the British blockaded the entrance to the Gulf from their bases in Newfoundland. A seven-ship French convoy — six of which belonged to the royal fleet — hastily departed from Québec and headed for France. One of the ships, the *Corossol*, ran into a storm and sank at the entrance to the port of Sept-Îles, not far from the island and lighthouse which today bear the ship's name. Aboard the doomed vessel were the wife and eight of the children of Jean-Baptiste-Louis Franquelin, the French king's hydrographer.

The struggle for control of the St. Lawrence and its entryway continued, culminating in the construction of a French fortress at Louisbourg, Nova Scotia, in 1719. In 1733, a lighthouse was built there — the first on Canadian soil. For nearly 25 years, the Louisbourg light signaled the end of the great Atlantic crossing, guiding ships into what would soon become the trading hub of New France. In 1758, the British attacked

Louisbourg for a second time. The French ships were hemmed in, then sunk in the harbor. Today, divers can visit the wreck of the immense 64-gun *Célèbre*, sunk during the siege. Its once mighty guns litter the bottom of the ship but part of the main mast still rises from the seabed. The wreck of the 74-gun *Prudent* lies a little farther out in the bay. As the warships sank, the Louisbourg light went out forever, signaling the decline of the French regime.

Under the British, the St. Lawrence became an important transportation route. Maritime traffic increased, and so did the ships' tonnage. No longer content with the port of Québec by itself, many vessels now sought to deliver their goods directly through the first American ports in the Great Lakes region. Lighthouses soon dotted the route, the first being erected in 1810 not far from Kingston, Ont., near the source of the St. Lawrence. For a short interval, the river, especially in its uppermost reaches, became a contested frontier. Between 1812 and 1815, the war between England and the fledgling United States turned the St. Lawrence and the Great Lakes region into a battle zone of tension, as demonstrated by the many shoreline fortifications that were constructed during this period. The massive shipwrecks that were later discovered near Kingston — veritable wooden barriers — reinforced this violent history.

For the reminder of the 19th century, a different kind of conflict was waged on the St. Lawrence, brought about by a combination of technology and an increase in maritime traffic. As the volume of shipments grew — due to rapid population growth in the western part of the continent — the introduction of steamships pushed the old sailing vessels to their limit. This competition, intensified by the increasing number of ships on the river, resulted in more frequent accidents. The need for better navigational safety methods became paramount. Lighthouses proliferated, to be sure, notably in the more treacherous areas, but not fast enough to keep pace with the increased traffic. Shipwrecks occurred more and more often, ironically in the very places where lighthouses had been erected: more than 80 around Pointe-des-Monts (1830); roughly 30 on the reefs around Île

Rouge (1848); 10 in the shadow of the Île du Pot à l'Eau-de-Vie lighthouse (1861) and 15 at Cap-des-Rosiers (1858). The perilous waters along the southern coast of Anticosti alone – Pointe Sud-Ouest (1831), Pointe Est (1835) and Pointe Ouest (1858) – claimed more than a hundred ships. While some of the wrecks, such as those lying on the shoals at Île Rouge, have been washed away or disturbed by strong currents, others, like the *Signy* at Pointe-des-Monts, offer divers an impressive collection of virtually undamaged artifacts. Whatever their condition, these shipwrecks, intimately linked to the nearby lighthouses as they are, constitute a kind of cultural landscape of our maritime history. Enhanced by the accounts recorded by lightkeepers in their journals, these physical remains add a human dimension to our seafaring past.

While our relationship with the St. Lawrence may have evolved over the years, the river remains true to itself: Its often calm and majestic appearance belies its ever-changing moods, particularly in the area east of Pointe-des-Monts on the Côte-Nord, where it can turn deadly. The contemporary accounts kept by keepers of those lighthouses where countless shipwreck victims found refuge, attest to the unforgiving nature of the river and to the dramas that unfolded over time. While storms created their fair share of havoc, the river concealed another aspect that caused great human suffering. The banks of fog that veil our beautiful river, seemingly so romantic when accompanied by the sound of foghorns, have time and again proved lethal. In fact, two of the

On Anticosti, near the lighthouse at Pointe Sud-Ouest, a little graveyard recalls one of the many tragedies that occurred all along the river's course.

The graveyard of the Gulf guards its secrets. Only a few half-submerged wrecks have been explored, like the Mongibello beside Escarpement Bagot. A multitude of wrecks lie scattered along the Anticosti shore-line and elsewhere in the St. Lawrence. On Anticosti itself, you can either visit or observe – on foot or by diving – the Calou, near Pointe Ouest; the Wilcox, near Pointe Carleton; the Faillette Brown, at La Loutre; the Mongibello and, finally, the Eastmore, in the Baie des Goélands.

worst marine disasters in the history of the river, each one costing more than 1000 lives, involved fog. In 1711, eight British ships belonging to Sir Hovenden Walker's fleet ran aground at Île aux Œufs, north of Pointe-des-Monts, taking more than 1000 men to their deaths. Fog also caused the tragic collision between the *Empress of Ireland* and the *Storstad* in 1914, in which 1012 men, women and children drowned in less than 15 minutes. This horrifying tragedy is still memorialized at the Musée de la Mer, situated at the foot of the Pointe-au-Père lighthouse. Experienced divers can venture down to see for themselves the huge bulk of the *Empress* as she rests on her side in the cold, dark waters near Rimouski. The immense scale of the wreck is equalled only by the agony of the drama that plunged it to the bottom.

But lighthouses and other aids have helped make navigation on the tumultuous waters of the St. Lawrence much safer. Shipwrecks involving loss of life are now isolated cases. Today, the river is a pleasure: yatchsmen sail from one marina to the next, those of a romantic bent comb its beaches in search of the perfect sunset, nature lovers keep an eye out for whales and campers sleep on its banks so they can be serenaded by the sound of waves. While some lighthouses have been become popular refuges for holidaymakers in search of peace and quiet, and will therefore survive, many others, falling apart after years of neglect, risk extinction. Too often careless of our own history, we have lost the links to our maritime past. How many of us realize that lighthouses and shipwrecks were "eyewitnesses" to that past? As such they have a fascinating story to relate about our long association with the St. Lawrence. All we have to do is listen.

From Sainte-Anne-des-Monts to Carleton

The immobile and now extinguished prism at Pointe à la Renommée stands out in sharp relief against the rising sun. The little lighthouse, witness to many a storm, is finally serene. It has regained its "home port."

La Martre

By Andréa Neu

The lighthouse at La Martre, the jewel of the Gaspé coast, stands proudly on its promontory, two short steps from the local church. Its striking octagonal structure is exposed to the sun's caress and the bite of the wind. It is the only wood-frame lighthouse on the coast. An earlier structure, built in 1876, next to the keeper's house, fell into disrepair and was demolished in 1906 to make way for a more modern one, more solidly constructed, able to support the installation of a dioptric lighting system and its large rotating mechanism.

As far as its four successive keepers were concerned, the favorable location of the lighthouse — in the heart of the village itself — led them to christen it the "Cadillac of lighthouses," because the loneliness that normally accompanied their calling was not a problem here. Moreover, there was a time when the proximity of the lighthouse and the church aroused a degree of jealousy in the *curé*'s heart. Yves Foucreault is the present keeper of La Martre, and he grins as he says: "There were two highly respected personalities in the village: the priest and the lightkeeper. But you could always detect a sense of rivalry between the two men, because the priest had a great deal of trouble accepting the fact that someone else could be in charge of a building that was as high as the church steeple."

LATITUDE: 49° 12' 22" N ■ LONGITUDE: 66° 10' 17" W ■ MUNICIPALITY: LA MARTRE ■ HEIGHT: 19.2 METERS ■ HEIGHT ABOVE SEA LEVEL: 39.6 METERS ■ RANGE: 17 NAUTICAL MILES ■ FLASH: 30 SECONDS

Foucreault is a stocky individual with the appealing look of an old sea dog. Beard flecked with gray, twinkling eyes and an open, friendly expression, he's instantly likeable. He quickly grows animated whenever the talk turns to the subject of the lighthouse – "his" lighthouse, as some people imagine. "It's not *my* lighthouse," Foucreault objects. But the fact remains that it is owing to him that the La Martre light exists at all today. Between 1970

> "There were two highly respected personalities in the village: the priest and the lightkeeper. But you could always detect a sense of rivalry between the two men, because the priest had a great deal of trouble accepting the fact that someone else could be in charge of a building that was as high as the church steeple."

and 1990, in the name of economic necessity, a wave of neglect – indeed in many cases of demolition – battered Quebec's lighthouses. It was decreed that those expensive giants be replaced by simple steel towers, topped by smaller and more up-to-date lights. The demolition of the La Martre lighthouse, automated in 1968, seemed a foregone conclusion.

Above: At La Martre, there's a long-standing rivalry between the lighthouse keeper and the local curé *– a war between steeple and lantern, as it were.*
Right: Like a "king" on a chessboard, the lighthouse casts a shadow over the site at La Martre.

Aware of its priceless value, Foucreault launched a veritable crusade aimed at sensitizing the members of the Canadian Coast Guard. They finally relented and began to appreciate the key role they could play in protecting this historic structure. Demolition was staved off. Starting in 1981, Foucreault organized two campaigns for renovating the keeper's house and the lighthouse itself in order to turn them into tourist attractions. In its first year of operation, the revived lighthouse welcomed nearly 12,000 visitors. Then, in 1994, the Musée des phares opened its doors in the old "foghorn building" itself. There, the story of lighthouse development is on display.

Between 1970 and 1990, in the name of economic necessity, a wave of neglect – indeed in many cases of demolition – battered Quebec's lighthouses.

Yves Foucreault continues to watch over his beloved lighthouse. Not only does he understand the smallest features of its inner workings, he has become a walking encyclopedia of lighthouse lore. He shares his unique knowledge and passion with enthusiastic visitors who come from the four corners of the globe. The fifth keeper of the La Martre light is indeed someone special, a living legend in the lighthouse world, though he never thinks of himself in that way. One thing is certain, though: He is from now on inextricably linked to the history of the La Martre lighthouse.

Above: Yves Foucreault, face to face with the "eye" of the La Martre lighthouse, which he renovated himself. For 17 years, Foucreault has helped keep the lighthouse open to the public. Left: Foucreault watching over his "personal" lighthouse. He doesn't keep track of his hours and personally guides every visitor group.

Cap de la Madeleine

The origin of the name Cap de la Madeleine, christened Cap Montmorency by Jacques Cartier, is uncertain.

It stems from the early decades of the 17th century, when French colonists obtained royal permits to develop the first seigneuries. It is generally believed that Antoine Caddé established the seigneury of Rivière-de-la-Magdelaine in 1679, but another theory suggests that Denis Riverin, a navigator who arrived in New France in 1686, holds the honor. Three years later, the Comte de Frontenac, then governor of the new colony, awarded Riverin the right to establish a permanent fishing post at the mouth of the Madeleine River. Riverin decided to give the seigneury his mother's Christian name.

Before it tumbles abruptly into the river, the escarpment of the Chic-Chocs mountains traces a series of roller-coaster turns worthy of an amusement park. There is no better vantage point to view the natural nautical highway that is the St. Lawrence than along the cliffs bordering Cap de la Madeleine. Perched on a rock, a nature lover can spend hours on end watching the moving river as it almost lazily infiltrates the heart of the New World. In winter the spectacle takes on a hypnotic rhythm as ice floes crisscross the river. With the coming of summer, you can scan the water and try to imagine what is unfolding in the deepest parts of this vast ecosystem.

LATITUDE: 49° 15' 03" N ■ LONGITUDE: 65° 19' 32" W ■ MUNICIPALITY: SAINTE-MADELEINE-DE-LA-RIVIÈRE-MADELEINE ■ HEIGHT: 16.8 METERS ■ HEIGHT ABOVE SEA LEVEL: 44.5 METERS ■ RANGE: 20 NAUTICAL MILES ■ FLASH: 27 SECONDS

Erected on a finger of land, the Cap de la Madeleine lighthouse dominates the river.

At the bottom of an undersea valley, the St. Lawrence's powerful discharge – known as the Gaspé current – heads toward the gulf like a locomotive under a full head of steam. There it meets the open ocean and, propelled by its extraordinary force, diverges, then splits in two. The traveler along Highway 132 has no idea of these or any other phenomena that are taking place in that hidden world. This is the place, for instance, where a salmon ends a long return journey that began far out in the Atlantic and will end in the river of its birth. The map of this epic voyage has been imprinted on the salmon's genetic code, so its progress seems guided by remote control. Soon it will leave the mineral salt-rich waters of the St. Lawrence and plunge into the fresh waters of the Madeleine River. The impact of this transition on its metabolism – a transition controlled by hormones located at the base of its brain – should in theory be fatal. However, in the course of its voyage across unseen undersea continents, its anadromous fish cells are designed to help its body cross the fluid frontier dividing salt- from freshwater. Thanks to this metamorphosis, it will be able to perpetuate the survival of its endangered species after swimming up the longest salmon ladder in the world.

At the bottom of an undersea valley, the St. Lawrence's powerful discharge – known as the Gaspé current – heads toward the gulf like a locomotive under a full head of steam.

Seen from the top of the road, located to the left of the sandbar on the Madeleine River, the tubular steel lighthouse structure looks far too flimsy for its rugged surroundings. Put up in 1907, it replaced the original lighthouse, a round concrete pillar covered by painted roughcast. The Fresnel lens still operates and, every 27 seconds, its Cyclops eye flashes over the river. The site now has a recreational purpose, housing a café and small museum that relates the region's history. Apart from tourists, however, there are few visitors. "People here aren't interested in the lighthouse," complains Carole Giroux, who does her best, despite a meager budget and the depradations of wind and tide, to keep the buildings open to the public. Once you have climbed not one, but two ladders, you reach the lantern room. The panorama over the river looks as if it had been taken straight from the pages of a novel by Jules Verne. At any moment, perhaps, Captain Nemo's *Nautilus* may break to the surface. But in fact it's more likely to be a U-Boat, one of those German submarines that terrorized the St. Lawrence during World War II. At dawn on May 12, 1942, the U-553 torpedoed the *Leto*, a Dutch cargo ship, in the waters off Cap de la Madeleine. Twelve seamen lost their lives and the survivors were taken to the Pointe-au-Père lighthouse.

The sandbar at the Madeleine River. The river is highly prized for its sport fishing.

Pointe à la Renommée

After 20 years of exile in Québec City, the little Pointe à la Renommée lighthouse has reclaimed its own plot of land. Located 50 kilometers north of Gaspé, Pointe à la Renommée may have acquired its name in 1736 when a ship christened *La Renommée*, outward bound from the French port of La Rochelle, ran aground on the island of Anticosti. An even more tragic tale concerns the castaways who died of hunger there. Afterward, it became known as *Pointe de la Faim*, which the English-speaking residents of Gaspé mistranslated as Fame Point. In their turn, French-speaking Gaspesians renamed the place Pointe à la Renommée. Whatever the case, over the years the point and its little lighthouse have acquired a degree of fame. The first wooden lighthouse was erected in 1880, and its faithful keeper, James Ascah, took charge of the station from 1880 to 1913. In 1901, the Italian physicist Guglielmo Marconi launched the first transatlantic wireless message. In 1904, the Pointe à la Renommée station became one of the first transatlantic maritime telegraph stations in North America. The wireless transmission marked the start of a new era in navigation.

Until 1925, the sea was the only means of access to the point. Local fishermen caught cod in abundance, and established seasonal camps along the shores of the point. Pointe à la Renommée was the last such seasonal fishing village.

LATITUDE: 49° 06' N ■ LONGITUDE: 64° 36' W ■ MUNICIPALITY: L'ANSE-À-VALLEAU ■ HEIGHT: 15.5 METERS ■ HEIGHT ABOVE SEA LEVEL: 57.9 METERS ■ RANGE: FIXED LIGHT

In 1977, the lighthouse was removed and installed in front of the Coast Guard building in Québec City. However, a group of zealous Gaspesians

In 1904, the Pointe à la Renommée station became one of the first transatlantic maritime telegraph stations in North America.

led by Blandine Poirier, a resident of L'Anse-à-Valleau, organized a five-year battle to persuade the Coast Guard to return the little lighthouse to its proper home. On October 22, 1997, Blandine Poirier, Marianne Côté, Anne-Marie Curadeau, Priscilla Poirier and Dannie Tapp celebrated the return of "their" lighthouse, reviving the economy of a small village that was once a fishing port.

Above: Thanks to the tenacity of Marianne Côté, Blandine Poirier, Dannie Tapp and Priscilla Poirier (left to right) – popularly known as the "stubborn Gaspesians" – the little Pointe à la Renommée lighthouse was returned to its original site after a 20-year exile in Québec. Right: Detail of the lighthouse guardrail.

Cap-des-Rosiers

In the mid-19th century, Ireland faced a ruinous economic crisis that rapidly deteriorated into widespread famine.

Oppressed by the English government and incapable of providing for their families, three million Irish had no choice but to emigrate to North America. They crossed the Atlantic under great hardship, clinging to their dreams of a promised land while they did their best to put up with the appalling conditions of the voyage – rats, illness and a general state of squalor. Large numbers – already in poor health when they embarked – perished during the journey. Many of the survivors landed in Canada. It was during this period that the Kavanaghs came to Quebec. Like their countrymen at home, they were destitute and perilously close to starvation. In the early morning hours of April 18, 1847, one of the ships, the brig *Carricks*, struggled against a strong wind as it attempted to skirt a tongue of land stretching all the way to the Forillon peninsula. Ice, combined with violent squalls, thwarted the vessel's every effort. The coast loomed dangerously close. Suddenly, during a violent commotion of wind and water, the brig ran onto a sharp reef at Cap-des-Rosiers, ripping its hull wide open. In the rush to escape, 87 people drowned in the icy seas.

Today, atop the 34-meter-high circular tower, Gérard O'Connor scans the agitated, foamy water. His facial features resemble those of a Breton, although his name betrays his Irish roots. Every 15 seconds, the huge

LATITUDE: 48° 51' 22" N ■ LONGITUDE: 64° 12' 03" W ■ MUNICIPALITY: GASPÉ ■ HEIGHT: 34 METERS ■ HEIGHT ABOVE SEA LEVEL: 41.5 METERS ■ RANGE: 25 NAUTICAL MILES ■ FLASH: 15 SECONDS

The Fresnel lens of the Cap-des-Rosiers lighthouse combines refraction, reflection and polarity, thereby allowing a 1000-watt bulb to generate 4-million candlepower.

Cyclops eye of the prism pulses out emerald-hued flashes into the surrounding air, printing laser-like green lines on the twilight-darkened surface of the water. In the distance, the gulf looms so large it could easily be mistaken for the ocean. On the cape, the century-old lighthouse stands tall, a beacon of natural beauty and man-made invincibility — a reassuring sight for generations of seamen traveling in those treacherous waters.

Built in 1854 at a cost of $75,000 — a staggering sum at the time — the Cap-des-Rosiers lighthouse is an important symbol of Quebec's rich maritime past as one of the gateways to North America. The lighting and optical equipment alone — three meters high and made of St. Gobain glass — cost $38,000. Lit for the first time on March 15, 1858, the white light was then one of the most powerful in Canada, marking the entrance to the gulf for the benefit of large three-masted sailing ships. Of all the Gaspé

Left: Sunlight makes the Cap-des-Rosiers "diamond" sparkle. Its 2.7-meter prism is the tallest in Canada and resembles an enormous beehive.

coastal regions, Cap-des-Rosiers witnessed the greatest number of shipwrecks. The *Chippewa, Arabian, Indian Chief, Pékin, Douchfour, Carricks* and countless others, all perished in its vicinity. In 1871, the station was equipped with a telegraph to signal the arrival of transoceanic liners. By then, although the keeper still had to climb its 122 steps twice a day to check the light, he no longer had to carry the one and a half tons of oil it took to feed the Argand wick burner.

The light is now operated by electricity, its beam still traveling more than 25 nautical miles at night. The station was designated a historical monument in 1977, 345 years after Samuel de Champlain first marked the cape's presence on one of his maps.

By then, although the keeper still had to climb its 122 steps twice a day to check the light, he no longer had to carry the one and a half tons of oil it took to feed the Argand wick burner.

It's closing time. Outside the lantern room, visitors Nathalie Poulin and Brian Tissot of Sudbury, Ont., check the light rotations against their watches. Gérard O'Connor waits patiently, lost in thought as he scans the horizon, perhaps dreaming about his own forebears who were once guided by this very light.

Tourists have fun timing the light beams. Meanwhile, hand in hand and 34 meters below, a couple makes a tour of the lighthouse.

Lighthouses are more than just geographical landmarks. They are the last witnesses to a unique maritime tradition. Resembling a stone sentinel, bathed in an autumnal glow, Cap-des-Rosiers is a proud example.

Cap Gaspé

Like a giant index finger pointing toward the deep, the Forillon peninsula extends 13 kilometers into the Gulf of St. Lawrence. At its outermost limit, Cap Gaspé and a small lighthouse mark the beginning of a hiking trail that meanders for 4574 kilometers through the great Appalachian chain. In the chill of an early January morning, Nicolas Mercier calmly busies himself in getting his team together. The dogs paw the ground impatiently. Ready at last, Nicolas pulls up the hood of his down parka and, in a soft voice, as if he were speaking to a child, commands: "Okay, dogs, let's go!" The team takes off like a shot. Anticipating the abrupt departure, Nicolas jumps smartly on the ash runners of his sled. Man and dogs carve a neat furrow through the freshly fallen snow. On the way into the wilds, they hug the coastline, pass by Grande Grave, then the venerable Hyman general store. Propelled by a south wind, icy waves from the Baie de Gaspé lash the shoreline. The dogs put their hearts into the effort and, even though it's covered in ice, they are undaunted by the roller-coaster ride through the peninsula. Working in concert with the lead sled-dog, Nicolas effortlessly choreographs their progress, and does so with a gentleness surprising in a "musher."

Anse-Blanchette is empty of tourists at this time of year. Like phantom shapes, snow flurries dance between the buildings, disturbing the tranquillity of a panorama that is indelibly frozen in time. People lived here

LATITUDE: 48° 45' 03" N ▪ LONGITUDE: 64° 09' 45" W ▪ MUNICIPALITY: GASPÉ ▪ HEIGHT: 12.8 METERS ▪ HEIGHT ABOVE SEA LEVEL: 106.9 METERS ▪ RANGE: 12 NAUTICAL MILES ▪ FLASH: 5 SECONDS

With a smile on his face, Nicolas Mercier watches the sun set on Cap Gaspé.

during the 19th century, managing to get by on what the sea had to offer. Established along the coastline, these families counted their wealth in terms of the abundance of cod. For them, codfish were the gold standard. In those long ago days, the Cap Gaspé lighthouse served as a landmark, not only for fishermen but especially for the trading ships on which the catch was loaded, bound for Italy and Portugal. Erected in 1873, the lighthouse was initially equipped with oil burners and metal parabolic reflectors. It was refitted in 1890, and again in 1950, so as to comply with the demands of modern commercial navigation. The lighthouse still clings to the cliffside, overlooking the water from a height of 106.9 meters. Silent now, and no longer in use, it hangs on while the paint is peeled away by the grip of the wind. From now on it is a mute witness to the power of the elements, but still clearly visible from the open sea.

Like phantom shapes, snow flurries dance between the buildings, disturbing the tranquillity of a panorama that is indelibly frozen in time.

Night has already fallen on the cape when, his nose running, cheekbones reddened by the northeaster, Nicolas swings the dogs around the lighthouse. The octagonal white tower, built in 1950, melds into the snow. At the foot of the cliff, banging against each other like agitated sheep, ice floes swirl and bob in the current.

Right: Despite the biting cold and the wind blowing in from the open water, Nicolas Mercier heads out from Cap Gaspé with his dogs.

Cap Blanc

Perched high on the limestone cliffs facing Île Bonaventure, the little Cap Blanc lighthouse dominates the Baie de Percé. In summer, the diminutive structure that juts its nose toward the imposing bulk of Île Bonaventure is a popular stop for tourists, campers and hikers. It's not much of a tour, though — a couple of steps, and you'll have covered the site. From time to time, an occasional gannet will perch on it — resting between dives — before flying off toward Percé Rock.

LATITUDE: 48° 30' 04" N ■ LONGITUDE: 64° 13' 05" W ■ MUNICIPALITY: PERCÉ ■ HEIGHT: 11.6 METERS ■ HEIGHT ABOVE SEA LEVEL: 46.9 METERS ■ RANGE: UNKNOWN

Cap d'Espoir

At the outermost bounds of the Gaspé peninsula, Cap d'Espoir pierces the Gulf of St. Lawrence. Scattered along a secondary road leading to the sea, a few houses cling to the cliffs. Above the rock-strewn shoreline, about 15 meters high, is the small lighthouse itself, a commonplace concrete tower built in 1939, that makes the site look even more nondescript. In springtime, the cape is a favorite resting place for migrating birds — common murres, puffins and eider ducks come to stay for a while on the shoals that stretch to the cape. In summer, tens of thousands of oldsquaw ducks and even some harlequins stop for a well-earned rest. Built in 1873, the first lighthouse was used to point out the gulf channel to Gaspé fishermen and to the first transatlantic vessels, although the documented history of the cape dates back to the time of Jacques Cartier.

It is recorded that in 1711, Admiral Hovenden Walker, on the way to attack Québec, lost one of his ships off the cape. Since that date, to the delight of visitors, his angry ghost is said to light up the sky on summer nights.

On such evenings, when sea and sky converge at the horizon and the cape's bronze cliffs stand out against the blazing light, Raymond Laprise and Isabelle Annamaria thank heaven for having decided, in 1994, to

LATITUDE: 48° 25' 09" N ■ LONGITUDE: 64° 19' 01" W ■ MUNICIPALITY: PERCÉ ■ HEIGHT: 14.1 METERS ■ HEIGHT ABOVE SEA LEVEL: 25.5 METERS ■ RANGE: 17 NAUTICAL MILES ■ FLASH: 30 SECONDS

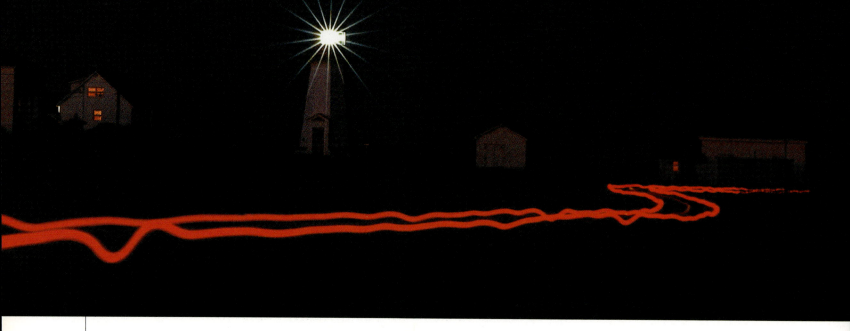

leave their home in the Laurentians to seek out a simpler life in the Gaspé.

At a turning point in his own career, Raymond has become keeper of the

Built in 1873, the first lighthouse was used to point out the gulf channel to Gaspé fishermen and to the first transatlantic vessels, although the documented history of the cape dates back to the time of Jacques Cartier.

symbolic lighthouse. The strangers he so warmly welcomes soon become

friends. From now on, their lives are regulated by the lighthouse beams

that once more cut across the Gaspé sky.

Right: Raymond Laprise and Isabelle Annamaria watch the sunset stretching out as far as the eye can see in front of Cap d'Espoir. Their dog, Candy, waits impatiently for suppertime.

Port-Daniel Ouest

Port-Daniel is one of the Gaspé region's main fishing ports. The village itself was named after a French sea captain, Charles Daniel, who sailed with Samuel de Champlain. Constructed in 1919, the small lighthouse, shining out over the waters of the Baie des Chaleurs, stands amid some of the oldest rocks on earth.

LATITUDE: 48° 09' 04" N ■ LONGITUDE: 64° 56' 59" W ■ MUNICIPALITY: PORT-DANIEL ■ HEIGHT: 10 METERS ■ HEIGHT ABOVE SEA LEVEL: 20 METERS ■ RANGE: 20 NAUTICAL MILES ■ FLASH: 5 SECONDS

Pointe Bonaventure

Founded in 1760, at a time when the battle of Restigouche was playing havoc with the surrounding countryside, the village got its name from a fishing boat called the *Bonaventure* that had foundered in the Gulf of St. Lawrence in 1591.

The first houses were built by the Acadians, but Basques, Normans, Portuguese, as well as people from the islands of Jersey and Guernsey, also settled down at the mouth of the Bonaventure River – sheltered by a sandbar – to fish the teeming waters of the Baie des Chaleurs. The battle of Restigouche was the last naval engagement of the Seven Years' War that had pitted the English against the French for the conquest of New France. French ships dispatched from Bordeaux, and loaded with reinforcements, to relieve Québec fell into English hands. They were unable to break through the English blockade and took refuge in the Baie des Chaleurs. Having got wind of their presence, the English went into action in late June 1760 and sank the *Machault*, a French flagship. The wreck was brought to the surface in 1972 and the archeological site, which took four years to excavate, was at the time the largest underwater research site in the world. The small, square lighthouse made of broad wooden planks was built in 1902 to warn fishing boats that they were nearing the point and to facilitate navigation throughout the bay. Now automated, the navigation aid is still in use.

LATITUDE: 48° 00' 15" N ■ LONGITUDE: 62° 26' 56" W ■ MUNICIPALITY: BONAVENTURE ■ HEIGHT: 10.4 METERS ■ HEIGHT ABOVE SEA LEVEL: 15.8 METERS ■ RANGE: FIXED LIGHT, NON OPERATING

Life-saving lights

Perched atop the towering structure, underneath a fireproof metal dome, the light – like a sparkling diamond – casts an intense, brilliant beam toward the dark horizon. A beacon of hope for mariners, a guiding star. How many shipwrecks did it help avert? How many lives did it save? A silent hero wouldn't dream of bragging about it. A lyric poet, on the other hand, just might.

Beginnings ▪ The earliest-known warning signals to guide seafarers at night may have been bonfires burning on the shore, crude lanterns flickering atop a cliff, or beacon fires maintained by monks. For daytime navigation, the early mariners relied on natural landmarks – a mountain peak, a rock, or grove of trees, for example – to find their bearings and reach their home port. While useful, these natural and fixed navigation aids left a lot to be desired. As maritime traffic increased, so too did the need for proper guidance systems. Markers, buoys, leading lights and lighthouses were gradually installed. In time, those navigation aids became more sophisticated, thanks in large measure to the Romans – renowned for their building skills – who erected lighthouse after lighthouse in France, England and Spain. In the Middle Ages, the activity began to slow down. Finally, most of the lights simply went out.

It wasn't until the 18th century that a renewal of sorts occurred, spurred on by the British, who erected a tower in the English Channel in 1698. France and Sweden soon followed suit. In fact, the French were credited with building the first lighthouse in Canada – at Louisbourg, Nova Scotia, in 1733. While all this was going on, Quebec remained in the dark. Finally, after 18 years of negotiations, a lighthouse organization was established – called Quebec Trinity House – and in 1809, the first light on the St. Lawrence went up on Île Verte. Others followed. The maritime route became safer, trading activities exploded, stimulating the country's economy still further. But how much do we know about these lighthouses? That their architecture varied in form and height, and their lighting apparatus reflected an ever-evolving technology.

Lamps ▪ In 1782, a Swiss inventor named Ami Argand (1750-1803) developed a lamp with a tubular wick in the shape of a hollow cylinder. An air current flowed through the cylinder, supplying oxygen to the flame, increasing its brilliancy. The resulting level of illumination was far superior to all the lighting mechanisms in use up till that point. Gradually, the new system was introduced in both private homes and lighthouses. By 1820, some 50 lights along the English and Irish coastlines were equipped with Argand lamps. Anxious to find ways of intensifying the light beam, scientists soon developed new methods and materials to refine

existing technology. The Swedes, for example, began to experiment with reflectors, in an effort to concentrate all available light and direct it in a particular direction. While ingenious, the light-reflector combination – known as the catoptric[1] system – was not entirely successful, because the reflector could reproduce only a small fraction of the light rays. It was a French engineer, J. Teulère, who eventually designed the ideal shape for the reflector, giving it a parabolic – rather than spherical – contour. Placed around the light source, the reflector captured all the light rays and focussed them in a narrow horizontal beam. The reflector-lamp made its first appearance in 1783. Another important development during this period involved the use of a clockwork motor to activate a continuously rotating mechanism that allowed the light (intermittent flashes came later) to sweep the horizon, where it could be seen by ships from any direction.

Next came Augustin Jean Fresnel (1788-1827), a French optics genius. Renowned for his experiments with lighthouse lights, Fresnel's first step was to replace metal reflectors with glass lenses. He soon moved on to study the ways in which light refracted and reflected. His observations led him to the multi-tier lens developed by the French naturalist and writer Georges Louis Leclerc Comte de Buffon (1707-1788). Fresnel refined the lens and, thanks to his ground-breaking contribution to the manufacturing process, the light refracted as it seeped through the lens' glass rings, casting its beam on the other side of the lens in parallel fashion. Thus the dioptric system was achieved. Not only was it capable of producing a light that was five times more intense than the old parabolic reflectors, it also projected a beam that was far superior in terms of intensity, range and precision. It was a giant leap forward as far as maritime-navigation safety was concerned. Later, the catadioptric principle was developed, combining elements of light refraction and reflection (lenses and prisms).

As the 20th century dawned, lighthouses quickly replaced their catoptric systems with the more efficient dioptric systems. Fixed lights, too, were gradually phased out in favor of flashing or occulting lights. With fixed lights, the light shone continuously at a constant intensity. With flashing lights, the flash itself only briefly illuminated the surrounding darkness. With group-flashing lights, flashes were grouped in two or more together, and occurred at regular intervals. With occulting lights, the periods of darkness between the flashes were briefer compared to the periods of illumination. As lamps changed and improved, so too did the type of fuel they burned. The first wick lamps operated on whale oil. But supply proved to be unreliable and rising prices soon limited its use. New lamps were developed that could operate on different types

1. *Catoptric,* from the Greek *katoptron,* mirror.

of fuel, such as colza oil, kerosene and, starting in 1900, coal oil and acetylene. In 1864, kerosene was the most commonly used light fuel in North America. Before electrification, there was of course no need for emergency lights. Lighthouses were therefore independent. In case of malfunction, an ordinary oil lamp with two flat wicks would do the trick. With the introduction of electric transmitters, however, emergency lights became indispensable. The La Martre lighthouse, for example, was supported by two large generators, one on top of the other, each containing 174 1.5-volt batteries. (Not all lighthouses were equipped with the same system). These generators are museum pieces today, because lighthouses are now equipped with solar panels that recharge their emergency-light batteries — a more cost-effective procedure. Fascinated and preoccupied with light since time immemorial, man has managed over the centuries to make light his ally — and an increasingly efficient one — in his long struggle against the elements.

Mechanism • Entering the enormous La Martre lighthouse, one is immediately struck by its beautifully preserved wooden structure. "The outside cedar shingles were all that was painted. The interior was left untouched, and this allowed the wood to breathe," explains Yves Foucreault, La Martre's current keeper. "In fact," he adds, "since the tower has never been heated or insulated, the wood remains intact." In the middle of the tower, a wooden column houses the old weight-and-cable system that once activated the light-rotating module. After a long search, Foucreault finally located the original plans detailing the system's clockwork mechanism, and was able to reconstruct it and get it working again. "The first visitors in the morning, and the last ones in the evening are the lucky ones," he says, "because that's when the system is switched on or off." In a matter of seconds, they've leaped backward 100 years. Most are astonished at how easy it is to make the two-ton lantern rotate — simply by pressing a button. In fact, the lantern itself does not rotate, it is the 12-liter mercury[2] basin in which it floats that does the turning — activated and controlled by the slow movement of the descending weights.

The rotating mechanism is similar to the workings of a grandfather clock. The length of time that a lighting module could rotate depended on the tower's height and the number of pulleys involved — details that varied from lighthouse to lighthouse. At La Martre, the 132-kilogram cable-and-weight system turns the module for three hours and

The complex bronze and glass assembly of Fresnel lenses constitutes a genuine work of industrial art. The manufacturing firms of Barbier, Bénard and Turenne in Paris, and Chance Bros. at Smethwick in the English Midlands, mastered the art to the point where they became the main suppliers of this equipment in the world.

2. There are two principles of rotation: using mercury or recirculating balls.

Detail of the ingenious set of gears that drives the lantern at the La Martre lighthouse.

45 minutes, obliging the old lightkeeper to wake up regularly at night to rewind the mechanism. Often, the operation involved the whole household — wife, children, assistant-keeper — each took a turn rewinding. Faced with such restrictions, one of the keepers eventually devised an ingenious system of warning bells that would awaken them 10 minutes before the deadline. In addition to rewinding and other daily chores, the keeper had to tend the mechanism itself — oiling, greasing and making constant adjustments to maintain accuracy and precision. In cold weather, for example, the grease might congeal, causing the mechanism to slow down. Time to add a small weight to the contraption to compensate for this shortcoming. The burner, too, required frequent checking. It was an incandescent mantle using vaporized kerosene, and its light was amplified by four Fresnel lenses. Used at La Martre until 1961, the burner was sustained by two demijohns, one for fuel — 20 liters (or five gallons) of kerosene that had to be replenished every other day; the other for compressed air. The demijohns, which still grace the lighthouse, were housed on the floor directly below the lighting apparatus, to keep them a safe distance from the flame. During the day, when the light was turned off, a white screen had to be drawn to prevent the sun from seeping through the lenses, and accidentally starting a fire. Seen from the river, the contrast between the vertical white strip and the red octagonal tower was striking — a clear, distinct landmark for mariners. As night fell, the keeper's work began. First, air had to be pumped in so the pressure could push the kerosene upward to the lighting module. Incidentally, each time the rotating mechanism was rewound, the keeper had to pump in more air to adjust the pressure. Next, he had to heat the burner before lighting it. To hear a keeper's daughter tell it: "The job was often infuriating, because the mantle would move, producing a thick black smoke that would soil the inside of the dome. That meant the keeper had to spend the next two days cleaning it. To deal with this less than cheerful prospect, especially if it happened in the middle of the night, one keeper dreamed up a scheme that automatically cut the oil feed and at the same time alerted him to the danger *before* too much damage was done. That little bottle of gin they kept in the armoire of the second-floor workshop came in handy, just to keep their spirits up."

No, a lighthouse keeper's job was not all fun and games. But keepers were a rare breed — self-sufficient, more devoted to their duty than they cared to admit, larger-than-life figures in the history of lighthouses.

Fog Signals ▪ Whenever dense fog conceals all visual landmarks, navigators rely on fog signals for direction. In the old days, bells, gongs, and even cannon were used, but the results were less than satisfactory. Sound did not travel well on water, and often gave misleading directions. Explosive devices were also tried, although the "bomb" – consisting of a gunpowder charge and a wick attached to one end of a long pole – was not exactly danger-free, at least from its user's viewpoint.

Canada's first steam-powered fog whistle was installed in the harbor at St. John, New Brunswick, in 1860. It was enthusiastically welcomed by sailors. Boasting an eight-horsepower engine, it produced a pressure of 100 lbs per square inch. Activated by a clockwork mechanism, the whistle emitted a 10-second blast every minute. In calm weather, the sound could be heard for 10 nautical miles. While efficient, it came with a cumbersome boiler and other machinery.

In 1899, a British-made fog whistle was installed on Belle-Isle, off the northern tip of Newfoundland. It consisted of an air compressor that was activated by a paddle wheel, and a double whistle for emitting sound signals. A rather similar system, called the Scottish steam whistle, was used at Louisbourg, Nova Scotia, and Pointe-au-Père, Quebec. These whistles produced excellent results, and continued to be used until a Canadian invention called the diaphone came along.

Designed in 1902 by J. P. Northey, a Toronto inventor and manufacturer, the diaphone was a modified version of the Scottish steam whistle. It proved to be an important development in fog signal technology, capable of producing a blast at a more even pitch while expending only one-eighth of the energy required to fuel the Scottish steam whistle. It worked on the same principle as its predecessor but used a slotted reciprocating piston rather than a slotted revolving rotor. The piston was actuated by a spurt of compressed air, which was stored in two or three large reservoirs. Larger diaphones were generally equipped with steam compressors, while smaller ones used the fuel variety. For its part, the foghorn, of equally imposing dimensions, could be positioned thanks to a fixed rail on a concrete base, but other modes of installation were also tested. As early as 1904, diaphones had replaced the old fog signals in all the main lighthouses in Canada and by 1929 as many as 153 diaphones were in use. The new apparatus required the services of a specialized attendant, and so a new position – fog-signal engineer – was created. Some experienced lightkeepers soon sought to qualify for the position, and were thus able to take on both jobs – plus two meager salaries.

Before lighthouses were electrified, different means of lighting were used, such as this kerosene wick lamp.

Light travels at a speed of 299,792,498 meters per second. With the advent of electricity, the electric bulb, combined with dioptric lenses, increased the power and range of lighthouses and helped save more lives.

In 1952, the development of a new resonator improved the diaphone's range. Eight years later, the introduction of the Airchine foghorn again placed Canada in the forefront of fog-signal technology. While it was not intended to replace the diaphone, the new device produced a signal of equal range at less cost. Its air compressors were activated by small electric motors and the entire apparatus was five times smaller than a regular diaphone. The first Airchine was installed in 1965. Pursuing its navigation-aid automation program, Transport Canada gradually replaced diaphones with electronic fog whistles. Another page was turned in the history of fog signals.

We have come a long way from those early sound signals, as well as the fascinating old-fashioned light sources and apparatuses. Electrification, automation and new technology have transformed navigation aids forever. Nowadays, with sophisticated technology such as the satellite-based GPS (Global Positioning System), a navigator's position can be plotted instantly, and so complicated calculations are no longer necessary. Lighthouses, once indispensable, have outlived their usefulness, and a centuries-old tradition is quietly fading away. Still, they have a lasting charm. The old structures will continue to stand guard, proud and unshakable. Some local groups now keep their lighthouses operational all year round, not just because of their universal appeal as tourist attractions, but also as a way of protecting an honored heritage and maintaining the tradition of offering refuge and safety to navigators. And if we should feel a twinge of nostalgia, solidly anchored as we are on terra firma, so too do mariners far out to sea, squinting at the horizon and rejoicing — just like their forefathers — at the sight of that reassuring light.

Anticosti Island

The Cap de Rabast light is promptly turned on as soon as the sun starts to go down.

Wilderness island

For 500 million years, an enormous limestone "ship" has been anchored between the Straits of Honguedo and Jacques-Cartier. At the azimuth of the cold air mass coming from the sea, and the mass of warmer air emanating from the earth, Anticosti lazily stretches out over 222 kilometers. Flanked by steep cliffs and surrounded by dangerous reefs, the island was once a sailor's nightmare, cut off by powerful currents and often shrouded in fog. It was dubbed the "graveyard of the Gulf." "Nowhere in the world have more shipwrecks occurred," Lieut. Henry Bayfield wrote in 1827 when he began to map the St. Lawrence for the Royal Navy. He recommended building two lighthouses at the eastern and western ends of the island. But Anticosti's dreaded reputation had already been established, and seamen's superstitions being what they are, a mere piece of equipment was not going to change matters. In his book, *Lightkeeping on the St. Lawrence: the End of an Era*, Normand Lafrenière wrote: "Although there have been three lighthouses on its south side since 1858, Anticosti still manages to put the fear of God into seafarers."

Despite the popular image of an inhospitable land created by tales of shipwrecks, mystery and witchcraft, Anticosti's rich resources and boundless forests have long attracted the attention of men willing to seek their fortunes.

Pointe Ouest

There are seven lighthouses on the island of Anticosti.

Close by the village of Port-Menier, the Pointe Ouest lighthouse was one of the biggest and most imposing of its kind in Canada. Imperially splendid in its coating of white, this 33-meter-high tower — rivaled only by its companion at Cap-des-Rosiers — was erected to face westward in 1858. Its 12-meter-diameter base is set firmly on a foreshore. Built of local limestone and faced with imported fireproof brick, its construction cost $50,000. Erected at the top of a stone stairway with 120 steps, a second-order rotary Fresnel lantern illuminated a 27-nautical-mile radius.

The lighthouse shone over the river until 1960. Battered by the elements, this splendid colossus with feet of clay slowly began to crumble. It was declared a hazard and, in 1961, the lighthouse was blown up. Now the most beautiful lighthouse in the gulf sprawls on the ground like a vanquished giant. Its scattered bricks are the sole reminder of its former glory.

LATITUDE: 49° 52' N ■ LONGITUDE: 64° 32' W ■ MUNICIPALITY: ANTICOSTI ■ ORIGINAL HEIGHT: 33.2 METERS (NOW DESTROYED) ■ ORIGINAL HEIGHT ABOVE SEA LEVEL: 34.1 METERS ■ RANGE: N.A.

Cap de Rabast

At the northern tip of Anticosti, suspended between sea and sky, Cap de Rabast looks across at the Mingan Archipelago. At low tide, you can head toward the reefs on foot and it's easy to imagine that the Côte-Nord is within walking distance. The 21-meter-tall lighthouse is surrounded by white-washed single-family dwellings and is used today as an outfitter's base. *Rabast* is an old French word meaning refuge. In the old days, it was the only place on Anticosti where ships could shelter from a storm.

LATITUDE: 49° 57' 05" N ▪ LONGITUDE: 64° 08' 57" W ▪ MUNICIPALITY: ANTICOSTI ▪ HEIGHT: 22 METERS ▪ HEIGHT ABOVE SEA LEVEL: 23.8 METERS ▪ RANGE: 17 NAUTICAL MILES ▪ FLASH: 30 SECONDS

Pointe Carleton

On October 26, 1768, Guy Carleton, Lord Dorchester, was appointed Governor General of Canada. In 1774, in an effort to improve relations between the English and French, Lord Dorchester lent his support to the passing of the Quebec Act, which guaranteed freedom of religion and the use of the Code Napoléon (the French civil code) for French-speaking Canadians. There is little doubt that he was one of the ablest English officials of his time. Today, Pointe Carleton on the island of Anticosti bears his name.

Located midway between the western and eastern ends of the island, facing the Strait of Jacques-Cartier, Pointe Carleton is one of Anticosti's loveliest sites. Built in 1917, its lighthouse is a classic, octagonal concrete tower. Ernest Carbonneau and his family looked after the station for many years until Eugène Francis took over. Sadly, Francis and his son were shipwrecked off Anticosti and both men lost their lives. Since then, the light has been automated and is still used as a navigation guide. Today, the old lighthouse station is a vacation center, offering nature lovers an awe-inspiring environment. Scuba-diving and guided nature tours are just some of the activities available. Not far from the point, the wreck of the *Wilcox* continues to resist the steady assault of the waves, as it has done since 1954.

LATITUDE: 49° 43' 53" N ■ LONGITUDE: 62° 56' 33" W ■ MUNICIPALITY: ANTICOSTI ■ HEIGHT: 12.2 METERS ■ HEIGHT ABOVE SEA LEVEL: 38.4 METERS ■ RANGE: 5 NAUTICAL MILES ■ FLASH: 6 SECONDS

Cap de la Table

It is barely sunrise at Cap de la Table. Inside the lighthouse – now transformed into a restaurant – the lantern shines on the still-wet grass. In the faint dawn light, camera clutched in his hand, a child stealthily approaches an unsuspecting bird. "If only I could crawl," the child thinks to himself, "then I'd have a chance to get close." He'd have slept on the ground with his good clothes on if he weren't afraid of upsetting his parents. Next, he starts zigzagging like a squirrel, hoping to get a picture of the bird before it flies away. Drying its wings in the emerging sunlight, the cormorant rests impassively on its perch. At last, after a series of wriggles and feints worthy of the last of the Mohicans on the trail of a wild animal, the youngster closes in on the roosting bird. The cormorant hasn't budged an inch. The boy raises his camera. Just as he is on the point of capturing the supreme moment of his holiday on film, his mother appears out of nowhere. She calls out in impeccable French: "Come and eat, Philippe! Breakfast is ready." Completely crestfallen, young Philippe finally realizes that the bird is just a piece of sculpted metal.

Anticosti Island

LATITUDE: 49° 21' 04" N ■ LONGITUDE: 61° 53' 44" W ■ MUNICIPALITY: ANTICOSTI ■ HEIGHT: 12.2 METERS ■ HEIGHT ABOVE SEA LEVEL: 34.1 METERS ■ RANGE: 5 NAUTICAL MILES ■ FLASH: 6 SECONDS

The reinforced concrete, fuselage-shaped lighthouse at Cap de la Table was erected in 1917. Its light no longer in use, the cape was eventually acquired by Safari Anticosti and turned into a tourist inn. Overnight, visitors can briefly experience what it was like to have been a lighthouse keeper before discovering, at a marathon runner's pace, the rest of Anticosti the following morning.

Drying its wings in the emerging sunlight, the cormorant rests impassively on its perch.

On April 19, 2001, Normand Duguay, MLA for the riding of Duplessis, announced that Quebec's council of ministers had endorsed the creation of an environmental park on Anticosti, centered around Cap de la Table. Eleven percent, or 91 square kilometers, of the area is henceforth under government protection.

There is hardly a living soul at Cap de la Table, at the tip of Anticosti. Then, all of a sudden, at a bend in the road, a resident fox trots nonchalantly by, while a hiker bumps into a cyclist.

Escarpement Bagot

Located near Bell River, one of the loveliest salmon rivers on the island, the Pointe Sud lighthouse was erected in 1912, primarily to indicate the presence of shoals. The site overlooks prime lobster-fishing grounds, and was once much favored by solitary keepers. The original light station, built in 1871, has disappeared. The current tower, a skeleton-like concrete structure supported by four buttresses, rises 15 meters high. Its lantern missing since the 1980s, the lighthouse continues to battle neglect — just like the steel wreck of the *Mongibello*, a half-submerged Canadian barge that lists forlornly in the water just a stone's throw from the lighthouse.

LATITUDE: 49° 03' 57" N ■ LONGITUDE: 62° 15' 35" W ■ MUNICIPALITY: ANTICOSTI ■ HEIGHT: UNKNOWN ■ HEIGHT ABOVE SEA LEVEL: 39.6 METERS ■ RANGE: NO LIGHT

Pointe Sud-Ouest

The turbulent north shore of Anticosti rises in marked contrast to the level and marshy coastline of its southern side.

In 1831, against all expectations, the southwestern tip of the island was chosen as the location for Anticosti's first lighthouse. Exposed to the four winds, and therefore visible to ships using the natural channel through the Strait of Honguedo, the 24-meter-high tower — the twin of its sister lighthouse at Pointe-des-Monts — housed the first rotary system on the river. Construction costs amounted to $34,000. Its lamps, using the oil of sperm and other whales as fuel, were visible at a distance of 15 nautical miles.

Nevertheless, ships kept running aground on the windswept coastline as the stark tombstones erected near the lighthouse bear witness: John Wright, drowned in October 1876; John Edgar Joyce, captain of the brig *Orient*, and his crew — Joseph and Stewart Taylor, Thomas Fitzpatrick, William Clark, Charles Henry, Ambrose Forward and Richard Taylor — all lost on November 22, 1874. Now these brave, vanished sailors have only the wind as visitor, accompanied by a few crows and the occasional fox that prowls around the lighthouse.

LATITUDE: 49° 23' 29" N ■ LONGITUDE: 63° 35' 40" W ■ MUNICIPALITY: ANTICOSTI ■ HEIGHT: DESTROYED ■ HEIGHT ABOVE SEA LEVEL: N.A. ■ RANGE: N.A.

People no longer visit the sombre precincts of Pointe Sud-Ouest. The problem is not just the two rivers one has to cross, that deters the visitors, but the old unsettling stories about the lighthouse itself. One Christmas

Nevertheless, ships kept running aground on the windswept coastline as the stark tombstones erected near the lighthouse bear witness.

Eve, it is said, the keepers burned it to the ground as they were preparing dinner. Ever since, the gloomy tower has stood alone in the midst of a wild meadow, like a solitary queen in the middle of an empty chessboard. But neither its massive crumbled stones nor the empty frames of its sun-scoured windows can obscure its beauty.

Like the leaning tower of Pisa, and now open to the four winds, the ageing queen of Anticosti offers a skeletal silhouette to those few visitors who dare to penetrate its core. A raging fire destroyed the magnificent wooden spiral staircase at the Pointe Sud-Ouest lighthouse, not to mention its light, its keepers and its very existence.

A tale told by Simon Gauthier, known as Simon of the River, based on a traditional Quebec folk story

The lighthouse keeper

Once upon a time, on an island in the middle of the St. Lawrence River, there lived a lighthouse keeper. Whenever dusk slowly shadowed the sky, that was the signal. The keeper started to oil his lamp wicks and, just as night was about to fall, he struck a match and tossed it behind him. The flame flared inside the huge lantern and sent its light skipping over the water. What a joyful moment, what better reason for living? The lighthouse keeper was so overjoyed when he saw his light pierce the surrounding darkness that, happy as a lark, he couldn't help breaking into song: "Round goes the light, and around go the boats! Round goes the light, and around go the boats!"

When fog shrouded the river and you couldn't see a thing, the keeper hauled out a big cannon. It was his foghorn. The report made an unholy racket, almost deafening and blinding him in an instant. "There's a fine line between heaven and hell," the keeper confided to himself. Then and there, he made up his mind to hire his brother, Ti-Jean, as assistant keeper. Nature had blessed Ti-Jean with intelligence and courage; it was for that very reason that the keeper took him on. And in short order, Ti-Jean set foot on the island.

As the weeks went by, Ti-Jean slowly realized that the lighthouse keeper reserved all the finest, starry nights for himself. Only when a whisper of fog floated down over the river was it Ti-Jean's turn to go to work. A miserable existence! Ti-Jean grew jealous of his brother. "One night, it's going to be your turn," he thought to himself. And sure enough, one fine day, Ti-Jean went to see his brother. "Listen," he told the keeper, "I've worked out our store of fish oil, and the wicks for the lamp, and we're soon going to run out. I'm going to cross over to Île Verte, then I'll row back toward Île Rouge, guided by your light. What do you think?"

"Ah, Ti-Jean, you're a bright fellow, and brave and smart into the bargain. So go ahead. The light will turn and the boats will go round. No problem at all."

Ti-Jean rowed away and the keeper was left alone in his lighthouse. He took his time arranging his chores and when dusk gently spread over the island, he said to himself: "It's time!" As he lit the wick, he couldn't help singing his little song: "Round goes the light, and around go the boats! Round goes the light, and around go the boats!" At that moment, the door flew open and there, bathed in the lamplight, stood a pirate. "Stop that infernal singing!" he barked. "I've heard it said, wherever I've roved on the open seas, that you were the happiest man in the world. So tell me your secret."

"Ah, Your Piracy, I'm delighted to welcome you here. But I don't have a secret. I've been happy since I was a little boy. What more can I say?"

"Keeper," the pirate replied, "are you actually telling me that you refuse to divulge your secret? Now listen carefully. Because of this affront, I'm going to ask you three questions. If your answers don't satisfy me by this time tomorrow, you're going to find yourself hanging high and dry from the yard-arm of my ship. You will tell me — one — how much I'm worth, I who have plundered countless ships. Two, how much the full moon weighs as it floats across the sky. And finally, tomorrow night, at the top of the tower, you must tell me what I'm thinking about. And remember, if your answers displease me, you're going to swing! So long, keeper."

The pirate departed, leaving the keeper alone again at the top of the lighthouse tower. Hunched over his table, he bemoaned his fate: "Please God! Please enlighten me. I beg you, Lord, let me have the answers." All night long he prayed and beseeched fervently. The hours crept by but he found no consolation — only groans and sobs. When Ti-Jean returned, his brother was still in tears. "What's wrong, keeper? I've known you for twenty years and this is the first time I've ever seen you cry. What happened? Your light goes round, the boats go around, you should be happy!"

"Ah, Ti-Jean. I was as happy as a lark and I sang my little song until the moment Red Beard the one-eyed pirate came to call," the keeper said, and proceeded to tell his brother about his unexpected encounter. "Tomorrow night, if my answers don't satisfy him, I'm going to hang." And the keeper groaned aloud.

"Oh, come on now, keeper, don't get into such a state. You know that I'm smart and intelligent. Tell me the questions and let's see if I can't help you out."

"But Ti-Jean, the questions are impossible to answer. The pirate wants to know how much he's worth — a man who has plundered countless ships. Next I have to tell him how much the full moon weighs as it sails through the sky. And the last straw — heaven help me — is how on earth am I going to tell him what *he's* thinking about tomorrow night?"

Ti-Jean listened carefully, and suddenly something clicked. His eyes lit up like the lighthouse itself — by now

extinguished by his brother's tears. "Keeper, stop crying," he said. "I've got it! This is what we're going to do. Take off your cap, your vest, your pipe and your suspenders, and give them all to me. I'm going to take your place." The keeper could scarcely believe his own ears. He thought Ti-Jean had gone mad. "But the hanging part, what are we going to do about that?"

"Don't worry about a thing, keeper. I'll take care of the pirate. You can go."

While Ti-Jean put on his brother's cap, vest, pipe and suspenders, the keeper left in a rowboat. He looked up at his big tower, and for the first time in his life, he saw that there was no light. He was filled with anxiety — those questions, the hanging, but especially Ti-Jean. The poor soul. What would happen to him? As for Ti-Jean, he wore a grin from ear to ear. At last, he had the lighthouse all to himself. He cheerfully waved goodbye to his brother, his petty jealousies hidden deep at the bottom of his heart. "Whatever you do, don't come back," he muttered, just loud enough not be overheard.

The night slid by under a starry sky. Ti-Jean took things easy, brought up the fish oil and oiled the wicks. He felt a happy tingling in his toes. He struck a match, burning his fingertips. But that was lucky, because the whole place could have gone up in flames. As Ti-Jean tossed the match behind him, the flame caught on inside the lantern and soon the light was waltzing over the St. Lawrence. His eyes were wide open, glowing like a red-hot stove. Happy as a lark, Ti-Jean couldn't help bursting into song, "Round goes the light, and around go the boats."

All night long, there was singing and there was dancing. Ti-Jean ran about inside the lighthouse like a rat on a treadmill. He behaved like a man possessed. He was happy at last. Daybreak came. If he hadn't been out of breath, he would have blown the sun away so the night would last forever. Unconcerned, the sun came up. "I'll keep the light turning anyway," Ti-Jean told himself. He didn't sleep, he didn't eat. He kept on singing, so too did the night birds. Just then the door burst open and there, standing in the doorway, was a man wearing a pirate hat and a pirate sword, fixing Ti-Jean with his pirate eye. It was Red Beard in person. He glared at Ti-Jean and said: "Keeper, if you don't stop that singing, I'm going to hang you on the spot, right here in your own lighthouse!"

Taken aback, Ti-Jean said: " Your Piracy, how nice of you to drop by. Do come in. As I told you yesterday, I'm the happiest man in the whole world. You can't stop me from singing."

"Very well, keeper! If that's the way you're going to behave. Listen carefully. I want to know right now – I, who have plundered countless ships, guided by the saints in heaven – how much do you think I'm worth?"

"You? Twenty nine shekels, not a penny more."

"What? That's not a lot, keeper."

"But Your Piracy, guided by the saints in heaven, Our Lord Jesus Christ was sold for thirty shekels. Even you can't be worth more than He was."

"That makes sense, keeper. I'm not worth more than Jesus. Now, my good friend, can you tell me the weight of the full moon as it moves through the sky?"

"The full moon? That's an easy one, Red Beard, it weighs one pound."

"Huh? One pound! Are you kidding the kindly old pirate? Have you got a screw loose? What are you talking about?"

"But Your Piracy, it's a well known fact that the full moon has four quarters. And four quarters equals a pound."

"That's logical. But now, keeper, here's my last question – the impossible question. You are going to tell me, Red Beard the pirate, what I'm thinking about at this very minute. Otherwise you'll swing from the yard."

"All right, Your Piracy, here's my answer. Right now what you're thinking is that the lighthouse keeper is answering your questions. But it's not. It's his brother, Ti-Jean."

You should have seen the pirate's face. His jaw dropped. Once he'd recovered his wits, he saluted Ti-Jean's intelligence. As he was escorting Red Beard back to his boat, Ti-Jean accidentally stepped on a mouse's tail. The little mouse went *Squeak, Squeak*, and that's the end of our story.

Îles de la Madeleine

Cap Alright shines out through the storm.

The windswept islands

Far from Quebec's shores, 247 kilometers off the Gaspé coast, a miniature country rises from the middle of the Gulf of St. Lawrence. It is called Îles de la Madeleine, the Magdalen Islands. Patiently, the dunes, the beaches of golden sand and sandstone cliffs the color of ochre, withstand the implacable elements. Here, there is no protection from the wind. It masters the land, as the land struggles against the sea. The 65-kilometer-long archipelago is often compared to a crescent or a fish hook, but in fact is more like a large and frail sandcastle dotted with lagoons. On its uplands, lush green grasses undulate in harmony with the swell of the sea. Here and there, small, boldly painted houses, showing all the colors of the rainbow, blend into a bucolic background. The ever-present sea and its shades of blue add a wild beauty to the landscape's palette. The inhabitants are Acadian to the core, hardy mariners and seal hunters. Look into their eyes, and the sea looks back at you. The islands represent the last bulwark against the encroaching ocean, the final refuge for sailors before the long crossing. Aware of their special place on earth, the inhabitants welcome visitors with open arms and a warm heart, whether they're expected or not.

After Jacques Cartier completed his first voyage in 1534, he paid a quick visit to the islands and christened them — with a touch of poetry — Les Araynes, derived from the Latin word *arena*, meaning sand. In 1626, Samuel de Champlain noted the name, Magdelaine, on a map as he was putting into the port of Havre-Aubert. But in the end it was François Doublet, the first *seigneur*, or lord, of the islands, who named them Madeleine in 1663, in honor of his wife, Madeleine Fontaine.

The islands are not unlike the tip of an iceberg submerged in the gulf millions of years ago. They conceal a myriad of dangers. The Micmacs and the Basques came here to hunt and to relax long before the arrival of the French, and their history is filled with excitement and drama. At the mercy of the ocean's currents, the caprice of the winds, the blankets of fog and the fluid motion of the sand, more than 700 ships have run aground or been shattered on these constantly shifting shorelines. The remains of broken hulls sometimes turn up on the beaches, as if to remind careless sailors and islanders — themselves seafaring men — of the importance of the lighthouses that flash along the perimeter of the islands. Rocher aux Oiseaux and its neighboring islands — Brion, d'Entrée, Cap-aux-Meules, Havre-Aubert and Havre-aux-Maisons — all have tales of shipwreck to relate.

The history of the lighthouses on the Îles de la Madeleine began in 1870 with the construction of a lighthouse on Rocher aux Oiseaux. Almost inaccessible, and isolated at the extreme northern tip of the archipelago in the middle of the Cabot Strait, the red sandstone rock – called Île Margauds by Jacques Cartier – is located at the entrance to the sea route up the St. Lawrence. Its steep, 30-meter-high cliffs are the cornerstone of the maritime graveyard that is the Îles de la Madeleine. In 1871 the lighthouse at Île du Havre-Aubert was constructed, followed by the light at Île d'Entrée, where descendants of Scottish and English settlers still live. The islands and their 9000 inhabitants, mostly Acadians, were in effect handed over in 1787 to Sir Isaac Coffin by the British crown. Next came the lighthouses at Île Brion in 1905, Cap Alright in 1920 and, finally Île du Cap-aux-Meules, in 1969.

Cap Alright

Standing all by itself in the dark of night, with the yawning expanse of the gulf before it, the little Cap Alright lighthouse looks vulnerable as it faces the storm-driven winds that assault it from every side. As if to make fun of its small size, white clouds diffuse its beams as they come to rest on its head. The Baie de Plaisance – or de l'Échouerie as it used to be called – is swept by waves from the Atlantic. That's where boats, driven by winds from the open sea, often came to grief. Survivors clung desperately to the furrowed sandbars, buffeted by waves amid the wreckage of their vessels. The lucky ones, rescued by the islanders, found a temporary refuge on one of the islands, sometimes even a wife and family, and many peacefully spent the rest of their lives there.

Îles de la Madeleine

LATITUDE: 47° 23' N ■ LONGITUDE: 61° 46' 02" W ■ MUNICIPALITY: HAVRES-AUX-MAISONS ■ HEIGHT: 8.3 METERS ■ HEIGHT ABOVE SEA LEVEL: 24.1 METERS ■ RANGE: 20 NAUTICAL MILES ■ FLASH: 5 SECONDS

Buffeted by the March wind, the Cap Alright lighthouse holds out against the biting winter cold and the lash of the Gulf's salt spray.

Cap-aux-Meules

A cold rain buffets Île du Cap-aux-Meules, disturbing the peacefulness of the summer day. All the same, the De Tilly family, together with their children and friends, have decided to make a quick tour of Cap du Phare. From the point itself, in spite of the flying spray, they can see Belle-Anse, its ochre-colored cliffs gnawed by the waves. After the traditional souvenir snapshot, everybody dashes back to the car. In summertime, the weather on the islands is usually milder. But the gulf has an unpredictable nature and, on this July afternoon, the scenic routes are imprisoned in a thick gray fog. As the local tourist board folk like to say: "On the islands, hospitality is just like Mother Nature, it doesn't depend on the calendar."

Îles de la Madeleine

LATITUDE: 47° 23' 05" N ■ LONGITUDE: 61° 57' 33" W ■ MUNICIPALITY: L'ÉTANG-DU-NORD ■ HEIGHT: 11.6 METERS ■ HEIGHT ABOVE SEA LEVEL: 29.9 METERS ■ RANGE: UNKNOWN ■ FLASH: 5 SECONDS

Île du Havre-Aubert

South of the Îles de la Madeleine, Île du Havre-Aubert stretches a sandy hook into the sea, cutting across the blue expanse that is the Baie de Plaisance. They say this is where the history of the islands began. Native people once lived here — traces of their presence are still visible — and this was where the first Acadians disembarked. The long shoreline — a genuine sand trap — is open to the ocean. Perched on a cliff just a few steps from the water, between Anse de la Cabane and Anse du Moulin, the lighthouse looks vulnerable to the next wave of erosion. In the distance, the green and secluded hills — the locals call them "Les Demoiselles" — form a round barrier against the cutting wind.

It was on that sandy hook, a short distance from the lighthouse, that the *S.S. Lunenburg* was beached on December 4, 1905, driven by a blizzard blowing in from the southeast. She was carrying freight and passengers between Souris, P.E.I., and Îles de la Madeleine. Many *Madelinots* lost their lives in that wreck, which occurred less than nine nautical miles from the port of Cap-aux-Meules, the *Lunenburg*'s final destination. Today, ships are no longer stranded on these shores, only the remains of sand castles are swept in by the tides.

LATITUDE: 47° 12' 44" N ■ LONGITUDE: 61° 58' 18" W ■ MUNICIPALITY: ÎLE DU HAVRE-AUBERT ■ HEIGHT: 17.1 METERS ■ HEIGHT ABOVE SEA LEVEL: 31.1 METERS ■ RANGE: 20 NAUTICAL MILES ■ FLASH: 20 SECONDS

The fields of wheat and canola that cover Île du Havre-Aubert wave in the July breeze. The wind blows ceaselessly on the islands, hardly ever changing direction.

Île Brion

The island girls are pretty, and Nadine Blacquière is no exception to the rule.

Blonde and bright-blue-eyed, with a siren's seductive smile, she guides tourists on Île Brion in the company of her captain. Twice a day during the summer, their eight-meter-long zodiac leaves Grosse-Île and, after a 10-mile crossing, sometimes calm, sometimes rough, the part-time Robinson Crusoes disembark on the magnificent beach at Île Brion. After checking in with the seasonal keeper, the visitors set off on a hike to explore the island's treasures. Once inhabited by several families, today Brion is a 650-hectare ecological preserve that has been protected since 1984. Rare plants such as *Hudsonia tomentosa* can be found on its sandstone cliffs, and there are primitive forests, peat bogs and hundreds of birds whose nests attract the attention of foxes. In the midst of stunted pines

Îles de la Madeleine

LATITUDE: 47° 46' 54" N ■ LONGITUDE: 61° 30' 30" W ■ MUNICIPALITY: GROSSE-ÎLE ■ HEIGHT: 13.6 METERS ■ HEIGHT ABOVE SEA LEVEL: 40 METERS ■ RANGE: 10 NAUTICAL MILES ■ FLASH: 3 SECONDS

Nadine Blacquière relates the history of Brion to a group of day-trippers who have come to follow in the steps of Jacques Cartier and the botanist Brother Marie-Victorin.

and tall grasses, the explorers, their picnics in their backpacks, take a winding path and follow in the footsteps of Jacques Cartier and Brother Marie-Victorin. Cartier named the island in honor of his friend and mentor, the French admiral Philippe de Chabot, Seigneur de Brion.

Once inhabited by several families, today Brion is a 650-hectare ecological preserve that has been protected since 1984.

The excursion will not continue to Rocher aux Oiseaux as planned. The pattern of the waves has changed and despite a blue sky, the captain's watchful eye detects the approach of a nasty southwest wind. Like the lighthouse keepers of old, the inaccessible island-sanctuary — today a refuge for seabirds — and its little isolated lighthouse will have to stand alone, exposed to the wind blowing in from the open sea.

Brion is an isolated spot, lonely and wild. In order to get there, you have to show your credentials and sign your name in a visitors' log, scrupulously maintained by the temporary park warden.

Bibliography

"Des sentinelles en voie de disparition sur mer et sur terre." Montréal: *La Presse,* 19 février 2000, p. H7.

La Gazette de Québec 1764-1874. Québec: Brown & Gilmore Ed.

La Presse. "Le taux de mercure est trop élevé dans plusieurs phares du pays." Montréal: 13 décembre 1999, p. C12.

BAIRD, David M. *Northern Lights. Lighthouses of Canada*. Toronto: Lynx Images Inc., 1999.

CANADIAN COAST GUARD. *Atlantic Coast List of Lights, Buoys and Fog Signals*. Ottawa: Fisheries and Oceans Canada, 2001.

CHARTIER, Jean. "Îles-de-la-Madeleine." Montréal: *Le Devoir,* 23 juillet 1998, p. B1.

CHARTIER, Jean. "Les phares du golfe du Saint-Laurent. Seuls dans la nuit." Montréal: *Le Devoir,* 28 mai 1998, p. B1.

COMITÉ DES LOISIRS DE L'ÎLE. "Île Verte. Avant-hier, au phare..." L'Isle-Verte-en-île: Les Éditions Lévesque-Langlois, 1990.

DESGAGNÉS, Hubert. "Le Haut-fond Prince." *L'Escale nautique,* avril-mai 1986.

DEPARTMENT OF CANADIAN HERITAGE. *National Historic Sites of Canada. History and Archeology.* Ottawa: National Historic Sites of Canada, 1972.

FAFARD-LACASSE, Élioza. *Légendes et récits de la Côte-Nord du Saint-Laurent*. Montréal: Antoine Lacasse, 1937.

FALLU, Jean-Marie. "Le rapatriement du phare de Pointe à la Renommée. L'identité retrouvée," *Continuité,* n° 77, été 1998, p. 47.

FRANCK, Alain. *Le Saint-Laurent 1900-1960*. Québec: Musée Maritime Bernier, 1980.

FRANCK, Alain. *Naviguer sur le fleuve au temps passé. 1860-1960*. Sainte-Foy: Les Publications du Québec, 2000.

FRENETTE, Pierre. *Le phare historique de Pointe-des-Monts et ses gardiens*. Québec: Société historique de la Côte-Nord, 1990.

GAST, René et GUICHARD Jean. *Les phares. Enfers et paradis*. Rennes: Éditions Ouest-France, 1999.

GAST, René. *Des phares et des hommes*. Paris: Éditions maritimes et d'outre-mer, 1985.

GINGRAS, Line. *Le phare de Pointe-des-Monts*. Québec: Direction générale du patrimoine, 1979.

GUICHARD, Jean et RENIÉ, Corine. *Phares*. Rennes: Éditions Ouest-France, 1991.

INTERNATIONAL ASSOCIATION OF LIGHTHOUSE AUTHORITIES, *Phares du monde / Association internationale de signalisation maritime, IALA*. Rennes: Éditions Ouest-France, 1998.

LAFRENIÈRE, Normand, *Lightkeeping on the St. Lawrence: the End of an Era*. Toronto: Dundurn Press Limited, 1996.

LAROCQUE, Paul. *Parcours historiques dans la région touristique du Bas-Saint-Laurent*. Rimouski: Groupe de recherche interdisciplinaire sur le développement régional de l'Est du Québec, 1993.

LAROUCHE, Marc. "Le phare de l'île du Pot à l'Eau-de-Vie désigné édifice classé du patrimoine fédéral." Québec: *Le Soleil*, 22 mai 1999, p. 63.

LEFOLI, Ken. *The Saint Lawrence Valley*. Toronto: Natural Science of Canada, 1970.

LEROUX, Maryse et HALLEY, Patrice. "Les Sentinelles du Saint-Laurent," *Geographica* (supplément de *L'actualité*), vol. 4, n° 4, juillet-août 2000, p.4-11; "L'exotisme à domicile," *Geographica* (supplément de *L'actualité*), vol. 3, n°4, juillet-août 1999.

MATTE, Gilles. *Carnets du Saint-Laurent* Québec: L'instant même, 1999.

NATIONAL GEOGRAPHIC SOCIETY. *Atlas of the World*. Sixth Edition. Washington, D.C.: National Geographic Society, 1990.

NATIONAL GEOGRAPHIC SOCIETY. *Field Guide to the Birds of North America*. Second Edition. Washington, D.C.: National Geographic Society, 1987.

O'NEIL, Jean. *Le fleuve*. Montréal: Libre Expression, 1995.

OUELLET, Yves. *Anticosti, l'île au large du Québec*. Laval: Éditions du Méridien, 1995.

PARISÉ, Robert. *Géants de la Côte-Nord*. Québec: Éditions Garneau, 1974.

PLISSON, Philip et al. *Phares Ouest. Les phares majeurs de l'arc Atlantique*. La Trinité-sur-Mer: Éditions du Chêne, 1999.

RAES, Daniel. *L'architecture des phares*. Saint-Malo: L'Ancre de marine, 1992.

RENARD, Léon. *Les phares*. Saint-Malo: L'Ancre de marine, 1990.

RUSSELL, Franklin. *The Illustrated Natural History of Canada. The Atlantic Coast.* Natural Science of Canada Limited, 1970.

SCHMID, Aline. "Saint-Laurent. Le long fleuve marin." *Thalassa,* n° 52, septembre 1991, p. 36.

TANOD, Lynn and JAKSA, Chris, *Guiding Lights. British Columbia's Lighthouses and their Keepers*. Madeira Park, B.C.: Harbour Publishing Co., 1998.

URQUHART, Jennifer C. "Scenic Shores of Quebec," from *Canada's Incredible Coasts*. Washington D.C.: National Geographic Society, 1991.

WITNEY, Dudley. *The Lighthouse*. Toronto: McClelland and Stewart Limited, 1975.

Acknowledgements

Special thanks to Jean Paré, then publisher of *L'Actualité*, and to Jocelyne Fournel, both of whom encouraged this project while it was still on the drawing board. My thanks to Gervais Bouchard of the Canadian Coast Guard for lending me "the key" to the lighthouses. In permitting access to all the sites, he gave me, perhaps unwittingly, the keys to paradise. Thanks also to Michel Couturier, to Roselyne Hébert and Patrice Poissant, of Tourisme Québec, for their involvement and logistical support. And a very special word of thanks to Bobby, for whom friendship is more than just a word.

Thanks to all those who, in one way or another, welcomed me to the lighthouses — on the north and south shores as well as on the islands — for transporting, housing, and sharing their knowledge.

Members of the Canadian Coast Guard: Georges Cossette, Herman Goulet, Bernard Lemieux, François Miville-Deschênes, Jean de Montigny, Raymond Renaud, Mireille Samson, Carl Vézina. Many thanks to Donald Moffet for his support and expert help with the technical and historical aspects of my research.

At Cap au Saumon, Cap de la Tête au Chien, Île Rouge and Haut-fond Prince: Robert Gilbert, Annie Goupil, Jean-Marc Darveau, Madeleine Lamarche, Alain Bossé and Diane Gauthier — those footloose photographers — Philippe Barry, Simon "du Fleuve" Gauthier, Martin Chouinard and Mylène Lamarche. At Cap Bon-Désir: Fannie Bernier, Marie-Hélène Fraser and Joanne Doyon. At Pointe-des-Monts: Jean-Louis Frenette and Eileen Yacyno as well as Herménégilde Comeau. At Île du Grand Caouis and Île aux Œufs: Sophie Lévesque, Marc and Elliot Blacquière, Christian Bouchard and the entire team of springtime kayakers. At Île du Corossol: Chantal Bouchard, Marcel Galienne and Gaëtan, of La Petite Sirène. At Île aux Perroquets: Danielle Kavanagh and her husband, Marius, Mrs. Marie Collin-Kavanagh, Christophe Buildin and Laura Del Giudice. At Petite Île au Marteau: Gilles Chagnon and Dominic Benoît, of Expédition Agaguk, Michèle Boucher, Cristina Martinez and Guy Côté, of Parks Canada.

On the island of Anticosti: René Tremblay and Air Satellite for travel assistance. At Pointe Carleton: the staff of Sépaq, especially Guy Element, Chantal Truchon, Sylvie Tremblay, Suzie Gosselin and Renée Martineau. At Cap de la Table: Jean-Marie Chrétien, of Safari Anticosti, and his lighthouse team at Cap de Rabast. And finally, Évelyne Noël, of Pourvoirie du Lac Geneviève.

At Île du Pot à l'Eau-de-Vie: Jean Bédard, Élize Lauzon, Marie de Blois, Paul-Louis Martin and all the down gatherers. At Île Verte: Gérald Dionne and Jean Cloutier. At Île Bicquette: Yvon Mercier, of Canadian Wildlife

Service, Marc Lapointe and Patrice Thibault. At Pointe-au-Père: Serge Guay and Michel Bujold. At Cap-Chat: Hélène Saint-Laurent and Sylvie Vallée. At La Martre: Yves Foucreault and Andréa Neu. At Cap de la Madeleine: Carole Giroux. At Pointe à la Renommée: Blandine Poirier, Priscilla Poirier, Marianne Côté and Dannie Tapp. At Cap Gaspé: Nicolas Mercier, Raynald Bujold and Denis Comeau, of Forillon National Park, and Gilles Shaw, of the Auberge de Cap aux Os. At Cap-des-Rosiers: Gérald O'Connor. At Cap d'Espoir: Raymond Laprise and Isabelle Annamaria. And lastly, my thanks to René Trépanier and Béatrice Joseph, of Québec Maritime, to Louis Rome and Christine Saint-Pierre, of the Association touristique régionale de la Gaspésie, and to Pierre Fraser, of the Association touristique régionale du Bas-Saint-Laurent.

At Îles de la Madeleine, thank-you to Claude Richard, of the Association touristique régionale des îles, and to the staff at Château Madelinot.

On the river, thanks first to Yves Pelletier and Jean Cloutier as well as the crew of the *Lovisa Gorthon*, then to Linda Jones and to the crew of the *L'écho des Mers*, of Écomertours.

Elsewhere, on land and in the air: thanks to André Leroux for taking good care of my SUV, and to my assistant, Solomon Krueger, for his cheerful spirits and for looking after transportation and equipment; to the lab team at Boréalis; to Manuel Damota, of Royal Photo, for supplying film and photographic equipment; to André Fournier, who showed me around the Gaspé; and to France Tremblay, of the program *Une bouteille à la mer*.

Without publishers willing to take risks, there would be no books in the first place. So a hearty vote of thanks to Pierre Bourdon and his team at Les Éditions de l'Homme. Thank-you to Joël Le Bigot for the foreword. Thanks as well to Marc-André Bernier, Jean Cloutier, Simon Gauthier, Maryse Leroux, Andréa Neu, Marie-Claude Ouellet and Pascale Pontoreau for their contributions. Thank-you to Philippe Brochard for his fine map. Finally, thanks to Ann-Sophie Caouette for designing the layout.

Thank-you to my daughter, Julie, for her willingness to spend the school holidays on the lighthouse journey.

And finally, thank-you to Maryse from the bottom of my heart. She tirelessly accompanied and supported me, organizing all my projects, and providing moral support. Without her, I'd be a mere shadow of myself.

Photographs and contributors

Photography, from the Greek words *photos* and *graphē*, means to write with light. All the photographs in this book were taken on Fujichrome film, using Hasselblad and Nikon equipment, with lenses ranging from 15 to 600 mm. Although most of the images were shot using natural light, I've sometimes used a flash or other artificial means, in conjunction with available light. Filters have been used sparingly, and only to heighten or coax out the existing light and color so they can be registered on film which otherwise would be unable to pick up the more subtle tones.

Marc-André Bernier ▪ Born in Kapuskasing, Ont., Marc-André Bernier has worked as an underwater archeologist since 1989, involved in various shipwreck recovery projects both in Canada and around the world. In the St. Lawrence River, he has led or co-led several projects, such as the *Corossol* and *Elizabeth & Mary* excavations, as well as others in the Saguenay/St. Lawrence Marine Park. He currently works for Parks Canada.

Jean Cloutier ▪ Lower St. Lawrence river pilot Jean Cloutier began his navigation career at the tender age of 17, later attending the Institut de marine in Rimouski, Quebec. He spent many years on Irving Oil company tankers, rising through the ranks from seaman to captain. He subsequently qualified for the two-year pilot apprenticeship program and in 1996 became a full-fledged river pilot, as his father before him.

Simon "du Fleuve" Gauthier ▪ Simon "of the River" Gauthier studied *Animation et Recherche Culturelle* at Université du Québec à Montréal (UQÀM), and today earns his living as a storyteller. In summer, he can be found in Tadoussac, and during the winter, in other parts of Quebec and in Europe. Named both "Ambassador of the Côte-Nord" (Grand Prix du Tourisme 2001) and "2002 Côte-Nord's Author of the Year" (Côte-Nord Book Fair), Gauthier has been nicknamed IMAX in recognition of his "3-D" style of storytelling.

Maryse Leroux ▪ Trained as a lawyer and translator, Maryse Leroux eventually turned her attention to journalism, in part as a way of indulging her passion for travel. Her language skills led to a reporting career in various parts of the globe. Her articles have appeared in both Canadian and international publications, such as *Geo Mundo, The World and I, Beautiful British Columbia, Doctor's Review, L'Actualité* and *Geographica*.

Andréa Neu ▪ A native of France, where she was a bookseller, Andréa Neu has been a *Québécoise* by adoption since 1978. One fine day in 1984, she "ran aground" on the Haute-Gaspésie shore, attracted by the rugged and pristine landscape of this isolated region jutting into the Gulf of St. Lawrence. It was at La Martre that she met Yves Foucreault, the lightkeeper to whom, in due time, she gave her own heart to keep.

Marie-Claude Ouellet ▪ After a stint as a naturalist in Quebec's Forillon National Park, Marie-Claude Ouellet, a biologist by training, is today a freelance science writer. In 1995, she received an award from the Association québécoise des éditeurs de magazines. Ms Ouellet is the author of *Le Saint-Laurent, un fleuve à découvrir* and *Fabulous Whales and Other Marine Mammals of Eastern Canada,* both published by Les Éditions de l'Homme.

Contents

Foreword	14
A brief history of the lighthouse	16
Map	22

From Québec to Tadoussac — 24
- Cap au Saumon — 26
- Cap de la Tête au Chien — 30
- Haut-fond Prince — 34
- Île Rouge — 40

Profession: St. Lawrence river pilot — 48

From Tadoussac to Sept-Îles — 54
- Cap Bon-Désir — 56
- Pointe-des-Monts — 60
- Île aux Œufs — 68
- Île du Grand Caouis — 72

From Sept-Îles to Blanc-Sablon — 76
- Île du Corossol — 78
- Île aux Perroquets — 82
- Petite île au Marteau — 92

The St. Lawrence — A river rich in resources — 96

From Québec to Saint-Anne-des-Monts — 102
- Île du Pot à l'Eau-de-Vie — 104
- Île Verte — 112
- Île Bicquette — 120
- Pointe-au-Père — 128
- Pointe-Mitis — 132
- Cap-Chat — 136

Shipwrecks and tragedies — 140

From Saint-Anne-des-Monts to Carleton — 146
- La Martre — 148
- Cap de la Madeleine — 158
- Pointe à la Renommée — 162
- Cap-des-Rosiers — 166
- Cap Gaspé — 174
- Cap Blanc (Percé) — 178
- Cap d'Espoir — 180
- Port-Daniel Ouest — 186
- Pointe Bonaventure — 188

Life-saving lights — 190

Anticosti Island — 196
- Pointe Ouest — 200
- Cap de Rabast — 202
- Pointe Carleton — 204
- Cap de la Table — 208
- Escarpement Bagot — 212
- Pointe Sud-Ouest — 214

The lighthouse keeper — 218

Îles de la Madeleine — 222
- Cap Alright — 226
- Cap-aux-Meules — 230
- Île du Havre-Aubert — 234
- Île Brion — 238

Bibliography	242
Acknowledgements	244
Photographs and contributors	246

Lithographed on Jenson 200 M paper and printed in
Canada at Interglobe Printing Inc. in March 2002.